EXAM S

John Croucher is Associate Professor and Head of the Statistics Department at Macquarie University, Sydney. He is the author of a number of business, mathematics and statistics textbooks, along with numerous scientific articles in international journals. He also worked as a television presenter for many years, offering football tips to desperate punters.

EXAM SCAMS

Best cheating stories and excuses from around the world

John Croucher

ALLEN & UNWIN

First published in 1996 by
Allen & Unwin Pty Ltd
9 Atchison Street, St Leonards, NSW 2065 Australia
Phone: (61 2) 9901 4088
Fax: (61 2) 9906 2218
E-mail: 100252.103@compuserve.com

National Library of Australia
Cataloguing-in-Publication entry:

Croucher, John S.
Exam scams: best cheating stories and excuses from around
the world.

ISBN 1 86448 165 X.

1. Cheating (Education). 2. Cheating (Education)—Case
studies. I. Title

Set in 11/13 Garamond Book by DOCUPRO, Sydney
Printed by Australian Print Group, Maryborough, Vic.

10 9 8 7 6 5 4 3 2 1

To the long-suffering students who
must endure the agonies of examinations
and the unfortunate markers who have
to read their answers.

CONTENTS

INTRODUCTION

A thing worth having is worth cheating for.

W.C. Fields

Examination time is challenging for both lecturers and students. On one hand, teachers dread the thought of having to set suitable exam papers, not to mention the gloomy prospect of numerous boring hours of marking. For their part, panic-stricken students are afforded the opportunity to display either a knowledge or ignorance of their subject.

For everyone, it is a time filled with apprehension. Seemingly, the only light relief comes from the attempts made by some students to bypass the normal exam process to gain that extra advantage that might just lift them over the pass mark or boost an otherwise ordinary performance. These devious or desperate individuals will go to great lengths to either provide a colourful explanation for their poor performance or, more commonly, for not doing the exam at all. Alternatively, they may take the opportunity to experiment with some of the vast range of cheating techniques known to students. In either case, it is left to the examiner to unravel the truth of the matter. This is not always easy.

Special consideration requests

There is a seemingly infinite variety of ailments that plagues students around exam time and many, suspiciously, manifest themselves only in the day or two of the actual exam period. Miraculously, the symptoms often disappear almost immediately the exams have been completed. Students who feel they have been disadvantaged can submit requests to the examiners for 'special consideration'—a term which covers any incident which was unforeseen or beyond the student's control. The special consideration proviso invites the creation of a dazzling range of misfortunes and the display by students of latent literary talents.

Common among exam-time tragedies are the full range of 'psychological difficulties' including depression, trauma, emotional instability, acute distress, mental fatigue, lack of motivation, anxiety, confusion and a general loss of interest in life. Such afflictions are difficult to prove or disprove, and so a deal of subjectivity and expenditure of precious time is involved in judging each case on its merits. On some occasions the student's request may even be accompanied by a note from a sympathetic counsellor supporting the student's position.

Even more common at examination time is the seemingly endless stream of physical ailments and injuries. To the forefront here are the popular one-day URTI (upper respiratory tract infection) or gastroenteritis medical certificates that just happen to coincide precisely with the day of the exam. These can suggest that the hapless victim was perfectly well on both the day before and the day after the exam but incapacitated on the actual day itself. Other favourite maladies include headaches, sore throats, sore backs, sore legs, chest or abdominal pains, ulcers and skin infections (or other unidentified rashes). Food poisoning and upset stomachs also play a prominent role.

More off-beat cases involve 'facial pains so that I can't think clearly' or excuses like 'I have suddenly developed RSI so that I can't write properly any more'. Some students even feel moved to overkill and put forward a host of problems— one, for example, stated she had 'nausea, fever, severe headache, backache, chest pains, watery eyes and giddiness'. It was a miracle that she could even write the letter.

Some cases readily arouse the suspicions of the experienced examiner. A cagey medical practitioner who suspects a fake illness might say 'Mr Jones came to my surgery today and said he didn't feel well', and leave the reader to their own interpretation. Some students will travel vast distances to obtain a one-day medical certificate from a particular doctor for an alleged minor ailment. They do this despite the presence of university doctors on campus only minutes away, whom they may visit free of charge.

Showing impressive versatility, students may claim to enjoy good health yet be so affected by other people's misfortune that their exam performance is severely hampered. Typical of this category are those who have to care for 'sick boy-friends/girlfriends' or who are related to someone currently in trouble with the police. Compulsory attendance at the funeral of a distant relative is also mysteriously common on exam day.

The reader should not be misled into thinking that there is a lack of sympathy on the instructor's part in considering any request for special consideration by a student. For example, in the 1995 New South Wales Higher School Certificate examinations involving about 61500 candidates there were 3963 appeals under its illness and misadventure provision and an overwhelmingly high 3415 (86 per cent) were upheld. On the other hand, four students had their marks reduced to zero in one exam while another was stripped of all marks in a subject as a result of serious breaches of the rules.

The vast majority of consideration cases are indeed genuine and are dealt with accordingly. Indeed, it does not stretch the imagination to believe some students when they declare that they 'developed a sudden headache when I saw the exam paper'. The ones that attract interest are those which are remarkable for their stupidity in either over-magnifying a trivial problem or creating difficulties when none exist.

Survey reports

The world-wide figures for cheating are worrying. A study released in 1994 of 2000 undergraduates in the United Kingdom found that more than half had cheated at university, including 2 per cent who admitted to seducing tutors to obtain better grades. The research, which lasted two years, found that 54 per cent of students admitted to paraphrasing other people's work while 6 per cent stole that of other students. There were 12 per cent who said they had copied answers from another candidate while 5 per cent had passed answers to others. Forty per cent claimed to have fabricated references at the end of their essays. Another common ruse was to hide vital reference books on the wrong shelves of the university library so that other students could not access them. In fact, one student in three admitted to this practice.

The survey also revealed that cheating was more common among science and technology students than arts and humanities students while other surveys place business students high on the list. It was reported that men cheated more than women, with pressure of time being put forward as the most common reason for cheating.

These results are not isolated and there are many instances over the years where surveys have revealed the extent of dishonesty at learning institutions. A survey by a research centre showed that 67 per cent of students polled at thirty-one colleges and universities in the United States admitted to some form of academic dishonesty ranging from using simple crib sheets to taking illegal hi-tech gadgetry into exams. A later Californian study of high school students revealed that two-thirds admitted to cheating in exams at least once that year alone. Other results have suggested that 25 per cent of students would lie to get a job, while 39 per cent of boys and 26 per cent of girls of high school age admitted they had stolen something from stores in the previous year.

Indeed, there have been recent reports of a United States industry of 'campus call-girls' who regard themselves as 'professionals' who will write students' essay papers for a fee. Some of these do so for a living, with the cost of writing a student's essay ranging from $15 to $20 (of which the writer gets half) per page. It is claimed that there is little chance of being caught since neither students nor markers read the essays closely.

Old methods

Many students still rely on the old favourite of smuggling crib sheets into an exam, while writing on arms and legs is also ever-popular. However, in an act of sheer brilliance, one student at an Australian university failed his subject after he inadvertently handed in notes he had used to cheat, along with his answers.

There are still cases of students engaging a more capable substitute to sit for the exam in their place, although this practice is now largely being eliminated by the use of photo identity (ID) cards which must be placed on the candidates' desks. This did not stop one enterprising business student, who substituted the imposter's photograph for his own on the card.

Signalling answers to friends during exams is still quite prevalent and there is a variety of techniques in fashion. These include using hands or feet, body movements, scratching various body parts, arranging items on the desk in a particular pattern, whispering behind pens, passing notes or talking in a foreign language.

Other innovative schemes that have stood the test of time are taping crib sheets under a desk, using a phoney name on the exam book to disguise ignorance, faking an illness and suffering self-inflicted wounds. Developing a 'sudden complaint' during an examination is a particular favourite.

The technological age

Hi-tech methods are on the increase, with radio transmitters concealed in pens, cassette recorders loaded with pre-recorded tapes and programmable calculators crammed with information all being found in examination rooms. In fact, even basic calculators have been used to conceal notes slipped under their covers, formulas scratched beneath their lids or material added to their instruction booklets.

A recent innovation experiencing skyrocketing sales is the calculator that can beam silent messages across the exam room, with some students describing it as the 'ultimate cheating tool'. As a result, for the past four years, Cambridge University has restricted candidates to the use of only one approved model of calculator. Other institutions either restrict models or purchase large quantities of calculators to hand out to students during examinations.

The call of nature

Toilet breaks are also convenient for the exam cheat and there are numerous examples in this book of an amazing range of activities undertaken in the cubicle, such as making mobile telephone calls, concealing notes behind the cistern and writing crib notes not only on the toilet paper and its inner cardboard roll but inside the toilet bowl itself.

One Sydney university department now hands out exam papers in sections that must be returned as completed if a student goes to the toilet. Other institutions have gone even further with toilet breaks basically banned—if you must go, then you are not permitted to re-enter the examination room. The only exception is a medical certificate that must clearly state that you have a problem in this regard. Not surprisingly, these measures have drastically cut down the frequency of toilet visits.

This book

Following is a collection of some of the more humorous and unusual explanations of poor exam performance and absence from the examination room, along with some of the more favoured cheating techniques.

Some examples are so lacking in imagination that they seem doomed to failure from the outset. However, others display a rare mastery such that they were actually successful or only uncovered by chance. These inspire a begrudging admiration for their ingenuity, but also a regret that the talented individuals involved did not apply their skills in a more productive endeavour.

The book is divided into three main sections. The first covers some of the popular cheating methods that I and my colleagues around the world have come across in our years of teaching, while the second outlines some of the more colourful excuses put forward at exam time. In these examples, the real names and faculties of students have not been used, but all the cases are genuine.

The final section comprises cases of cheating from around the world that were so outrageous that they attracted headlines. These are categorised according to the region in which they occurred and represent only a small selection of the material available.

Although the creativity of the characters portrayed in these stories can be enjoyed at one sitting, their cases may also be considered as a buffet where the reader can select one or more items at a time and really begin at any place without losing continuity.

There are, of course, many other examples that could have been discussed but space did not permit their inclusion. However, the selection on offer provides an indication of the antics of those who aspire to cheat the system and will also serve as a valuable guide for those whose aim is to catch them. In any case there is no doubting the entertainment value of cheats and we can only sit back and marvel at their inspired genius.

CHEATING STRATEGIES

Making mobile phone calls

Smuggling crib sheets

Concealing papers on the body

Tampering with ID cards

Self-inflicted injuries

Using fingernails

Stretching exercises

Using previous exams

Impersonating the lecturer

Using a thesaurus

Desk arrangements

Sitting for exam twice

Plastic bottles

Baseball caps

Taping notes under desk

Tearful confessions

Handing in blank sheets

Copying from third parties

Blaming markers

Using relatives

Creeping

Feet movements

The importance of being mobile

Well-informed people know that it is impossible to transmit the voice over wires and, that were it possible to do so, the thing would be of no practical value.

Boston Post, 1865

The hi-tech age has certainly had an effect on the level of sophistication shown by those who are prepared to side-step the exam system.

For example, during a particularly harrowing accounting exam, Kate felt that drastic measures were required if she were to have any chance of passing. Accordingly, about thirty minutes into the exam, Kate asked if she could go to the toilet. This normally presents no problem and candidates are accompanied by one of the supervisors to the outside door of the toilet to ensure that it is indeed their destination.

On this occasion, however, after about fifteen minutes of waiting outside, the supervisor decided to investigate the

delay and entered the wash-basin area. She was quite alarmed to hear a vigorous conversation in progress, since she was sure that Kate was the only person using a toilet.

Indeed this was the case. From the comfort of her cubicle, Kate had managed to telephone a friend on her mobile phone and obtain the answers to the exam questions that she fed down the line. Her biggest mistake was to take too long and arouse suspicion or she may well have succeeded.

Kate's short-term university career came to an abrupt end soon afterwards.

Pray for help

Some things have got to be believed to be seen.

Ralph Hodgson, poet

Sean knew the examination rules quite well. In fact, he had been suspected of exam cheating before, but nothing could be proven. Feeling particularly lucky, he decided to secure assistance in his history exam by means of notes carefully scripted on a piece of paper.

The exam got off to a cracking start and Sean easily managed to slide the paper to and from his sleeve. It was only after an hour or so that the supervisor spied the offending crib sheet. It was unfortunate for Sean that, unnoticed, she made a hasty bee-line for his desk.

He looked up to see the looming figure only several desks away and the sheet lying incriminatingly in front of him. In desperation he scooped it up and crumpled it into a small ball. With impressive split-second timing he then thrust it down the front of his jeans. When challenged by the supervisor to hand it over, he blatantly refused on the grounds that it contained 'a personal message' that was nobody else's business.

Sensing potential disaster, the supervisor was unwilling to retrieve the paper herself. Instead, she allowed Sean to complete the exam and reported the incident later to authorities.

At the subsequent disciplinary hearing, Sean maintained that the paper had been a 'religious icon' which had given him comfort through what he knew would be a difficult exam. To everyone's surprise, he produced what he alleged was the article in question—a crumpled piece of paper containing a religious picture.

The committee was divided in its view of the incident and the only punishment Sean received was a 'severe reprimand'. He passed the exam.

Exam smuggling

All you need in life is ignorance and confidence and then success is sure.

Mark Twain (attrib.)

For accounting students, a high spot in the examination period occurred when Rita submitted a medical certificate two days before the exam. As luck would have it, she was able to find a sympathetic medical practitioner who was prepared to testify that, owing to acute gastroenteritis, she would be quite unfit to sit for her two auditing papers. It would be necessary, therefore, for her to sit make-up exams later.

It was common knowledge among students that, if a make-up exam was administered within a few days of the original, then the paper set was invariably the same. Indeed, so it would have been in this case except for the diligence of other students.

While distributing the question papers for the first exam, preoccupied supervisors failed to notice a supposed examinee who picked up two copies, one of which he placed under his jacket. At the conclusion of the exam, so as not to draw attention to himself, he handed a paper in along with the other students. He was noticed because he was not enrolled in the course.

When the smuggling incident was reported to the dean by two concerned students later that day, one stated that she was firmly convinced that the stranger was a friend of the missing Rita. After a description of the culprit was circulated to invigilators, officials were on their guard in case he turned up to the second exam. And sure enough he did.

However, rather than apprehend him at this stage, they allowed him to repeat his earlier performance and walk out with a copy of the second paper. There was little doubt in anyone's mind that Rita would be confidently spending the next few days busily researching the answers to what she assumed would be her make-up exams. But her plan was to end in failure.

The dean had instructed the accounting lecturers to hastily devise two completely new auditing examinations, neither of which bore any resemblance to the original. Rita was asked to sit for them both on the same day and, owing to her ignorance of the material, she met with little success and her results were a predictable disaster.

At a subsequent inquiry at which she was invited to explain events, she confessed that she and 'a boyfriend' had arranged a supposedly foolproof scheme which had badly misfired.

Rita refused to name him but it scarcely mattered since after her two failures she dropped out of college.

This incident also caused the college to abandon its practice of setting make-up exams the same as the original.

The great impostor

Money can't buy friends, but you can get a better class of enemy.
Spike Milligan, Puckoon, *1963*

Ravi was a struggling economics student, quite unhampered by the talent necessary to obtain a passing grade in his final exam. Attendance was checked at the exam by means of a student identity (ID) card, enclosed in plastic and containing

a photograph of the candidate. Candidates leave their cards on their desks during the exam so that supervisors are able to match the photograph with the person sitting in the chair.

With alarming ingenuity, Ravi managed to find an impostor who, for the sum of $500 (US$370), was prepared to sit for the exam in his place. Presumably he was convinced that his accomplice would have a better chance of passing the paper than he would. The difficulty of the photograph was easily overcome by carefully slicing the plastic ID coating and placing a photo of the substitute on top of his own.

The scheme initially worked quite well since the supervisor did not notice anything amiss. However, the situation deteriorated when Ravi's absence was noticed and several of his fellow students later reported a stranger doing their final examination.

Initial questioning of Ravi by examiners was treated with stubborn resistance and a fierce denial of any wrongdoing. However, a subsequent comparison of handwriting, a threat to call in the police and further grilling led to a complete confession. The name of the substitute, though, will never be known. Ravi claimed that he was 'some student I met in a pub a few days before. He said he knew something about economics but I never got his name.'

Ravi was expelled.

A nose for trouble

Circumstances alter faces.

Carolyn Wells

Since he was blessed with only a minimal understanding of physics, Kevin was somewhat apprehensive about his upcoming examinations. Precariously placed on the border-line of a failing grade, he knew that a poor final exam performance would sink him. It occurred to him that his chance of success would be significantly enhanced if he had more than one opportunity of sitting for the examination.

His carefully devised plan of action seemed foolproof and, to his credit, was carried out with military precision. After the papers were handed out to the candidates, it took Kevin only a few minutes browsing to realise that he had no chance of correctly answering sufficient questions to pass.

With split-second timing, when the supervisor briefly had his back turned and Kevin was confident that the other students were busy with their own exams, he drew back his fist and punched himself fairly on the nose. The predict-able deluge of blood was carefully directed to maximise the damage to both the question and answer papers.

As is the case with 'unexpected' nose bleeds, Kevin was spared further distress and was quickly ushered to a sick-bay for recovery. There was no question of his completing the paper at this time.

Given another opportunity, Kevin studied sufficiently in the following four weeks to manage a marginal pass, both in the make-up exam and the course. A friend later confided that this was not the first time Kevin had successfully tried this stunt and managed to exploit his 'weak nose'.

Good grooming

It is only shallow people who do not judge by appearances.
Oscar Wilde, The Picture of Dorian Gray, *1891*

To her friends and lecturers, Caroline was a very pleasant and always smartly dressed woman whose classwork could be considered mediocre at best. To everyone's surprise, however, she seemed to have the uncanny knack of performing above herself in examinations. Her lecturers put this down to a good memory and skilful exam technique, but it was only after she graduated that one of her girlfriends felt moved to reveal the secret of Caroline's success.

Along with her impeccable dress sense, it transpired that Caroline had beautifully manicured fingernails which were extremely long and the subject of some admiration from those who compulsively chewed their own from time to time. They had, however, a sinister use. Before an exam, Caroline would write copious notes on long, narrow strips of paper that she would carefully roll up and place under her fingernails where they were completely concealed.

Choosing the right moment during an exam, Caroline would unravel the strips, use the information, roll them back up and replace them.

She was never caught.

Sleeping on the job

When a man tells me he's going to put all his cards on the table, I always look up his sleeve.

Lord Hore-Belisha, Secretary of State for War, 1937-40

Although Chris and Paul were good friends, there was no question that the latter had a superior knowledge of financial practices. They decided to use their relationship to advantage during their final accounting exam at business college. They arranged the seating so that Chris sat directly behind his friend.

Their plan was perhaps too ambitious. For the first few minutes Paul attacked his question paper with relish, writing furiously. From time to time he deliberately looked up at the supervisor and, with a slightly embarrassed smile, yawned while placing his hand over his mouth.

To the uninitiated Paul looked nothing more than an unfortunate student who had stayed up too late studying the night before. However, it was not long before the yawning became more pronounced and his arms began stretching out to the side on each occasion. Soon enough, the arm-stretching graduated to exaggerated movements behind his head, and an occasional slight tilting of his chair backwards.

Since this charade was repeated about every ten minutes, the supervisor's suspicions were soon aroused. Without warning, she sprinted down the aisle and stood behind Paul after a vigorous stretch. On the desk behind him, occupied by the startled Chris, were little folded cards. Not surprisingly, these contained trial balance sheets and equations relating to the exam paper.

By previous arrangement, Paul had agreed to drop behind him any hints that he thought might help his companion. This technique may well have worked, except that he made the mistake of trying it too often and becoming too obvious by grossly over-acting.

Both Paul and Chris were given a year's suspension from their studies to get their act together.

A change is as good as a holiday

Conscience gets a lot of credit that belongs to cold feet.

Anon.

In teaching institutions, exam papers are kept confidential until they're handed out in the exam room. Some lecturers take such an enormous pride in the questions they have set that they insist that students also return their question papers after completing the exam. This is done to prevent their widespread circulation and allows some lazy staff to shirk the hard work of thinking up new questions for the next time.

At one college, the lecturing staff in mathematics were so impressed with their final exam paper that they used exactly the same questions two years in a row. They had worked quite well in discriminating the good students from the weak, so staff saw no reason to change them. The exam was used for a third time.

It was about 5.30 p.m. two days after the final exam that a distressed student identifying herself as Alicia knocked on the door of the department head. Alicia explained that she had seen a copy of the maths exam a week prior to its sitting date—apparently it had been circulating among the students in the dormitories. Alicia described herself as an honest student who wanted to obtain her grade fairly and had wrestled with her conscience for over a week before coming forward.

The head at first thought the claim was ridiculous since the examination papers were kept under tight security in a strong room with a combination lock. Nevertheless, further investigations and interrogation of other students revealed that there had indeed been a paper circulating beforehand and it was evidently identical to the one which was set.

It was estimated that over 100 of the nearly 500 candidates had seen the paper, although it was impossible to identify all of them. After much soul-searching, the college took the unprecedented step of insisting that everybody sit another final exam, despite the threat of legal action from some of the more indignant students. This new paper was, of course, completely different to its predecessor.

The offending exam paper was never sighted by the administration, although there was little doubt that it existed. How had the students obtained it? There are many theories, but the explanation given by several students is a strong possibility.

Once the same exam has been used for two years in a row, or there is a suspicion that a lecturer has a habit of not changing exam questions, the student grapevine quickly exploits the situation. Students agree to each memorise one question. When the exam is over, they leave the room and write down their allotted question before they forget it. These questions are collated and typed up with the following year's date.

When the exam is next offered, the students either sell or circulate their paper as the real one. Usually their version is extremely close to the original and there is no shortage of buyers.

In view of the severe disruption and embarrassment caused on this occasion, staff at the college were banned from using the same exam questions again, no matter how brilliant they might be. It must also be remembered that of all the students who had been party to prior knowledge, only one came forward. Had she not done so the practice would have continued.

When a stranger calls

A celebrity is a person who works hard all his life to become known, then wears dark glasses to avoid being recognised.

Fred Allen, comedian

Apart from examinations, one of the more unpleasant aspects of student life is the drudgery of homework. Any innovative technique to escape the tedium is always welcome, especially if it can guarantee excellent results.

Since most homework, especially in the quantitative areas such as mathematics and other sciences, is set from the textbook, an ideal companion for a student is the manual containing the solutions to every problem in the book. The difficulty is that these are only made available to genuine lecturers in the subject area.

Such an obstacle did not deter an enterprising business student whose identity still remains unknown. Around 10 a.m. on a Tuesday morning during term, a smartly dressed man aged in his mid-twenties appeared at the reception counter of a well-known book publisher. He identified himself as 'Dr Bill Johnson', a recently appointed lecturer in economics at a nearby college.

He explained that he was seriously considering adopting one of the publisher's textbooks for his course, and although he had the book itself he did not as yet have the solutions manual. Since he was passing by it seemed like an ideal opportunity to pick one up so that he could make his final decision. Would they be able to get a copy for him quickly since he was running late for his lecture that morning?

Things appeared to run smoothly until the receptionist politely asked for some kind of identification for their records. Sheepishly, the imposter ruefully explained that he had left his wallet in his car that was parked several blocks away.

Sensing trouble, the suspicious worker asked 'Dr Johnson' to wait while she allegedly went to retrieve the required manual. Instead, she rang the college to verify his credentials, only to find that such a person did exist but was at that moment sitting in his office.

Unfortunately, when she returned to reception, the villain had disappeared, apparently having got cold feet. He was never identified.

However, there have been occasions when students have successfully obtained the treasured solutions manual. At one college, some accounting students were caught reproducing an incorrect solution to a particular problem in their homework. In this instance the hapless students had been set a problem for which the solution provided by the manual contained several typing errors. When challenged, they admitted that they did indeed have a copy of the manual but refused to say how they had obtained it.

Word power in action

A guilty conscience is the mother of invention.

Carolyn Wells

Word processors have been a godsend to those of us whose handwriting is illegible or who are simply incapable of neat presentation using a pen. Expert in their use were Richard and Emma, good friends who were both enrolled in a business law course. Of the two, Emma possessed far more talent.

The major essay for the course carried a weight of 40 per cent of the assessment and the studious young woman duly completed her effort in plenty of time, meticulously presented with the aid of a computer word processing package. Richard was so impressed with her work that he took the opportunity, when Emma wasn't looking, of removing from her bag the diskette containing the file of her essay.

With inspired cunning he loaded it into the same computer program that Emma had used and soon had her file on the screen. Using the thesaurus capabilities of the program, Richard proceeded to randomly pick out words and phrases and alter them by making substitutions using synonyms. When he was finished, the basic structure of the essay was the same but the actual word content differed. Unnoticed, he slipped Emma's diskette back into her bag.

Despite there being about fifty students in the course, the astute marker had a feeling of *déjà vu* when assessing Emma's effort, having seen Richard's several papers before. After placing them side by side, it was obvious that some degree of copying had taken place, although the source was hard to identify.

When the students were called into the dean's office to offer an explanation, both denied any collusion whatsoever. It was only when they were threatened with six months' suspension for cheating that Richard's conscience got the better of him and he decided to confess to save the innocent Emma. He was punished while she was exonerated.

Sleight of hand

Some people will believe anything if you whisper it to them.
Louis B. Nizer, Thinking on Your Feet, *1940*

One of the more popular methods of examining nowadays is the multiple choice exam in which candidates are given choices of usually four or five answers to questions from which they must select the ones that are correct. (These are also popularly referred to as 'multiple guess' exams!)

This method of examining is especially prevalent in courses with large enrolments as exam papers can be marked using optical scanning devices. Multiple choice papers are also a favourite of some students, who find them particularly easy to cheat in.

Some examinations are so well supervised that it is difficult to pass notes or whisper to other students without running a grave risk of being caught. However, an effective means of communication during multiple choice exams involves the use of signals. Although hand signals may be used, they are likely to attract attention and are considered too risky. Instead, messages are passed by means of the arrangement of pens, erasers and rulers on desks. Simple codes are pre-arranged by students and memorised before the exams.

For example, if a pencil placed flat on the desk in front of a student has the sharp end pointing north, this indicates an answer of 'a', pointing east indicates an answer of 'b', south indicates 'c' and west indicates 'd'. The question number to which the answer applies is determined by the positioning of other pencils or pens. For example, two pens together followed by a space and then another pen could indicate question 21.

In this way answers are passed around the exam room without being detected by the supervisors. This technique was revealed to staff at one college by a graduating student who expressed amazement that the administration had not known about it since it was so widespread.

An interesting variation on this technique is for students to use coloured M&Ms (small candy-covered chocolates) on their desks to signal answers. Different colours stand for different letters or have a pre-arranged numerical value. Moreover, this method has the advantage of edible evidence—if supervisors become suspicious or even just when the exam is over.

What's in a name?

If all economists were laid end to end they would not reach a conclusion.

George Bernard Shaw, (attrib.)

On some occasions a course contains so many students that the lecturer is obliged to examine the students in shifts. This might mean, for example, that half of the students do an exam on one day and the remainder undertake another paper at either a later time that day or even the next day. For the most part, these exams are usually not exactly the same but, for consistency of ranking students, are similar.

This heartening state of affairs confronted Natasha, a mediocre economics student. Natasha was one of those who elected to do the exam offered on the first day. After spending two hours writing her exam and basically getting nowhere, she decided that she was really capable of a much better effort. The problem was that the test papers were not only collected but that the candidates' names were checked off so that it wasn't possible to sit for both exams.

A solution to this dilemma soon became apparent to Natasha and she decided to write the name 'Elton John' on the front of her answer book. When the exam finished she handed in her effort secure in the knowledge that there would be no record of her ever sitting for the paper. The plan was to return the next day and do the second exam under her real name, having looked up the answers to questions she hoped would be asked again.

In a way the plan worked, since Natasha's effort in the second exam was extremely good. However, since there was no 'Elton John' enrolled in the course, it was clear to the examiner that somebody else must have written in the phoney answer book on the first day. It was clear that the culprit was a student who did not wish to be identified.

With admirable tenacity the examiner placed 'Elton's' paper on the desk and proceeded to compare 'Elton's' handwriting with that of all the students who sat on the second day. Since Natasha's handwriting was easily recognisable, it was not long before the truth was uncovered.

After feeble attempts at denial, the threat of bringing in handwriting experts was enough to break Natasha's resolve and a full confession followed. Her career as an economist was put on hold when she received an automatic fail grade and six months' suspension.

Tune in for the latest

Baseball is almost the only orderly thing in a very unorderly world. If you get three strikes, even the best lawyer in the world can't get you off.

Bill Veeck, US baseball executive

It is not unusual for students (male and female) to wear baseball caps while attending lectures or even undertaking examinations, and generally supervisors have raised no objection. Indeed, some students feel that a cap is an essential part of their everyday wardrobe and although this may be somewhat bewildering to the older generation, there are usually no rules preventing attire of that kind.

One such student was Patrick, who looked splendid in his bright orange and green cap with matching jacket. However, it was not his clothing that attracted the attention of the elderly supervisor of his final-year marketing exam. Rather, every few minutes Patrick would place his left hand in his jacket pocket and, after a few seconds, remove it.

Careful scrutiny by the supervisor made it clear that the hand in question was empty both when it went into the pocket and when it came out. On the surface it seemed to be just another peculiar mannerism, but after about forty minutes of numerous action replays the supervisor took decisive action.

Patrick was asked to remove both his cap and jacket and it was then that the intrigue was unravelled. In his left pocket there was a cassette tape recorder. Attached to this was a wire that passed through a small hole cut in the bottom of the pocket, passing up his back, under his cap and finally to his left ear. The earpiece was concealed by Patrick's hair.

On a cassette tape Patrick had pre-recorded numerous hints, phrases and facts that he felt would come in handy during his exam. The hand movements were to play, pause, fast forward and rewind the tape as necessary.

Although secretly admired by some for his inventiveness, Patrick found himself repeating the exam six months later, this time without his colourful wardrobe.

Planning ahead

A kleptomaniac is a person who helps himself because he can't help himself.

Anon.

In order that invigilators know exactly where each student is supposed to be sitting, it is not unusual for candidates to be assigned a specific seat in a final examination. This also enables absentees and imposters to be easily identified.

It was left to Anwar, appropriately a business major, to turn these stringent measures to an advantage. After diligently checking his room and seat allocation for a finance exam to be held in several days time, he wasted no time in preparing his master plan. This involved the writing of copious notes on crib sheets and placing them in a brown envelope that was left open at one end with the flap removed.

With his exam due to commence at 9.30 a.m., Anwar correctly predicted that the room would be unlocked and unattended late on the previous afternoon. He stealthily crept to where he would be sitting and taped the envelope under the desk so that the sheets could be easily slid in and out for his perusal during the exam. He was confident that his parcel would not be detected before the morning and that he could simply remove it the following night.

To his credit, the plan almost worked since his scheme was not uncovered by supervisors during the exam. Unfortunately for Anwar, however, a student sitting nearby became incensed by his antics and reported them to examiners later that day. It did not take them long to confirm the nature of the cheating when they retrieved the envelope before the unfortunate Anwar had the opportunity to get there.

Anwar was unable to offer a suitable explanation for the existence of the envelope, especially since it contained sheets covered with his handwriting, and he quickly confessed. Far from being contrite, he seemed rather proud of his scheme. It had seemed to him to be such a good idea that he had been unable to resist giving it a try. He was suspended for one year.

An attack of conscience

I can resist everything except temptation.

Oscar Wilde, Lady Windermere's Fan, *1892*

Cheating in exams is not a field in which everyone can excel, and this was certainly the case with Anthea. This nervous student was particularly apprehensive about her upcoming mathematics exam since she was painfully aware of her lack of ability. Indeed, she found her predicament so disheartening that she decided that it would be necessary to seek the assistance of crib sheets that contained the formulae essential for success.

Anthea soon got down to the serious business of writing out a number of formulae on several pieces of paper and carefully slipping them up the sleeve of her blouse. At home she painstakingly rehearsed removing and replacing them until she was confident she could do so without detection.

The big day came, but Anthea's enthusiasm for the plan had waned as time progressed. Nevertheless, she found herself sitting in the examination room with the notes concealed in her sleeve. However, as the test papers were being distributed, her feelings of guilt and fear finally overcame her. Although she was sorely tempted to peek at the crib sheets, all she could think about was what might happen if they were detected.

Her positioned worsened and she became totally gripped by panic and unable to put pen to paper or, for that matter, even move, since she felt sure that the sheets would be discovered. So she just sat there.

After some time, a supervisor noticed the immobile student and asked if there was a problem. Much to her own relief, Anthea blurted out a confession on the spot. At her subsequent disciplinary hearing, an unsympathetic panel failed her in the course and administered a severe warning, but refrained from suspending her.

The invisible man

History is bunk.

Henry Ford, giving evidence in a libel action, 1919

Many institutions set exam papers for which the candidates must write answers in special booklets. The procedure is that each student is initially given only one of these blank booklets but will be supplied with more upon request. Each examinee is required to fill out an attendance slip so that supervisors can certify who sat for the paper and check handwriting if there is any suggestion that an impostor was present.

In a carefully conceived manoeuvre, Max decided that such stringent conditions could work in his favour in a history paper that he was quite sure he otherwise had no chance of passing. Along with the other candidates, Max duly filled out his attendance slip which was collected before the candidates commenced writing.

During the exam time itself, however, Max wrote nothing. He sat there holding his pen and pretending to write so as not to attract the attention of the supervisor, but his booklet remained blank. At the end of the exam the students were asked to ensure that their names were on the front cover of their answer booklets and to place them on the front desk as they walked out. When Max's turn came he simply placed his blank booklet in the pile.

When the examiner marking the scripts came to the blank booklet, he simply assumed that it had been put there by mistake and put it aside. All the other papers were marked and the grades recorded. Max was awarded a 'failed absent' grade. Full of righteous indignation he stormed up to the department head and pointed out that indeed he had been present at the exam; a fact that could be easily verified by checking the attendance slips. Clearly the examiners had lost his exam booklet!

The examiner was confused. A frantic search failed to reveal any sign of the 'lost paper' and with Max threatening legal action and refusing to sit through 'another harrowing exam', the college found itself in an awkward position. Since it was apparently the fault of the examiners that Max's paper was lost, it was agreed that Max should receive an automatic pass in the subject. Of course, Max gratefully accepted.

Max's ruse was revealed by a friend of the culprit after both had graduated. However, the tale's authenticity was impossible to prove.

When strangers meet

A friend in need is a friend to be avoided.
Lord Samuel, British Home Secretary, 1916 and 1931–32

It is not unusual for a lecturer to be faced with marking two supposedly independent essays that are essentially identical. The task of solving the crime by enticing one or both of the authors to confess is not pleasant.

Such was the situation when distressingly similar economics essays were submitted by Pauline and Larissa. The lecturer found the situation somewhat disturbing, since at no time had she seen the two suspects in each other's company during their university studies.

When the students were summoned before the dean to explain the 'coincidence', both vigorously denied even being acquaintances and swore that they did not copy from one another, as alleged by the authorities. Indeed, both said they would attest to this fact in court if necessary.

So convincing was their performance that they were believed. This was only to be expected, since they were telling the truth. In that case, how did they come to submit identical essays?

The solution was simple. When first one—and then the other—student confessed, the authorities discovered that they had not copied from one another, but instead each had paraphrased the essay of a mutual friend who had written on a similar topic in the previous semester. Neither Pauline nor Larissa was aware that the said friend had lent her essay to anyone else and both were genuinely surprised when they were apprehended.

The pause that refreshes

Once, during Prohibition, I was forced to live for days on nothing but food and water.

W.C. Fields

Displaying a previously hidden talent for ingenuity, Roger entered the engineering exam armed with a full plastic bottle of a well-known brand of raspberry-flavoured mineral water. After feigning several coughs at the exam door, he explained to the supervisor that it would be necessary to have the occasional sip during the exam so that his coughing would not annoy other students. To emphasise the point, he added that this water was the only nourishment that he was allowed in his present condition.

After a cursory inspection of the bottle, the supervisor readily agreed to Roger's request. The exam commenced without incident with Roger taking the occasional sip through a straw and not attracting much attention. However, in a procedure known in some circles as 'snappling', this fine student had previously removed the label from the bottle, written copious formulae on the back, and glued it back on.

Of course, the formulae could not be seen while the bottle was full of red-coloured liquid, but once the level was reduced sufficiently, the contents could easily be tipped to reveal the required information on the 'crib-sheet' label. Amazingly, Roger was not caught. His scheme, however, was disclosed somewhat later by a fellow student, by which time it was too late to prove anything. It was revealed that Roger had successfully used this ruse on a number of occasions.

The aggrieved student

The object of all psychology is to give us a totally different idea of all the things we know best.

Paul Valery, TelQuel, *1943*

Angela had always found psychology to her liking but was completely lacking in ability when it came to passing the section of the course that involved statistical work. Moreover, she was painfully aware that a fail grade in the statistics component would see her excluded from further studies in her chosen major.

During her first year, Angela learned from a friend the process of 'switching'. This could take several forms, the most common being as follows.

1 After the papers have been graded and returned to the students, a dishonest student may erase or cross out wrong answers and write in the correct answers. The student then challenges the marker as to why answers have been marked as incorrect. (It helps if answers were written in pencil.)

2 A dishonest student might leave out sections of a question altogether and write in the correct answer after the exam booklets are returned. The student then demands to know why the answer was not marked. (In this case no tell-tale crossing-out of the wrong answer is required.)

3 A variation of method 2 involves neglecting to answer whole questions then, when the answer booklet is returned, writing the correct answers in the back of the booklet several pages after the previous last answer. The student then confronts the markers and explains that they must have missed noticing the answers since they obviously assumed that they had marked everything attempted. The answers were in the back of the booklet because the student tried those questions first and did not know exactly how much room to leave for the other questions before them.

In this case, Angela relied on technique number three. The day after receiving her failing grade on an exam paper which had been returned to her, she carefully wrote out the correct answers to several statistics questions which she had not attempted during the exam toward the back of her booklet. She knew that good marks in these questions would lead to a pass.

Showing a deal of unconstrained confidence, Angela made an appointment with the professor in charge of the subject during which she indignantly showed him the exam booklet which had been returned to her. She remarked at length on the carelessness of the marker who had dared to fail her due to incompetence at missing her answers. The professor listened intently and appeared to nod sympathetically until her tirade was completed. He immediately summoned the marker to his office and showed him Angela's paper with the unmarked questions.

Far from being chastened, the marker produced a number of pages of his own which he had carefully stapled together. They were, in fact, a complete photocopy of Angela's unretouched answer booklet, including blank pages, which he had witnessed by a colleague. Not surprisingly, the newly found answers were not recorded on the marker's copy.

Angela could sense her position worsening since she was unable to account for the sudden appearance of the unmarked answers. It was explained by the marker that he had heard from a colleague that Angela had successfully tried 'switching' in another subject and at the time had been given the benefit of the doubt. He was determined not to be another victim and was taking no chances.

As a result of this clever detective work and Angela's subsequent confession, she failed the course and was given six months suspension.

A baffling puzzle

It has always been desirable to tell the truth, but seldom if ever necessary.

A.J. Balfour

Mystery surrounded the case of two students who handed in what appeared to be almost identical answer papers for their final mathematics exam at a high school. The marker had no difficulty in uncovering the collusion since the submissions had identically incorrect graphs and working-out for various problems. Nobody else in the class had answers remotely approaching what he discovered on their papers.

Sensing an early resolution because he was aware that the two suspects, Deborah and Barry, were girlfriend and boyfriend, the marker checked the exam seating arrangements, fully expecting that they would have sat either at adjacent desks or one behind the other. However, he was startled to learn that Deborah had sat in the back seat of one row while Barry was near the front of the class several rows

away. He felt there was simply no way that they could have exchanged answers during the test.

Other teachers were brought in for their expert opinion since it was considered preferable to be able to present the alleged culprits with strong evidence of guilt to ensure a confession. Despite their many suggestions, nobody could come up with a method that could have been used, particularly to transmit identically incorrect graphs. This meant that if both students vehemently denied cheating, it would be very difficult to prove.

After three weeks of fruitless speculation and with the end-of-year holidays imminent, it was decided to confront the pair one at a time. At this stage the main motivation was curiosity, since the teachers were keen to uncover the plot in case others also tried it.

If both students had steadfastly denied cheating, then they would have escaped. However, as luck would have it, Deborah broke down and confessed almost immediately. She and Barry had not collaborated during the exam itself. As the teachers had expected, that would have been impossible under the circumstances. What the authorities had not known, however, was that the school caretaker was Deborah's uncle and that the cheating took place after the exam.

On the day of the exam after the teachers had all departed, the caretaker kindly let his niece and Barry into the staff-room where they busied themselves in altering their exam answers to make sure they agreed. Such was their confidence in their joint ability that they apparently did not check anyone else's paper.

Both students were suspended and the helpful uncle was dismissed.

Drive carefully

We all know what happens to people who sit in the middle of the road. They get run over.

Aneurin Bevan

An interesting variation on the way in which answers can be passed around an examination room was provided by Bernard who had successfully used this technique in a number of multiple choice exams. It is sometimes known as the 'stick-shift' method. It was only some time later that Bernard's trick was revealed by a 'friend'.

The process involves the use of feet and it is handy, although not essential, for the users to be familiar with the gear-shift mechanisms of manual cars. In pre-arranged manoeuvres, if the left (or right) foot is placed in 'first gear', the answer is 'a'; 'second gear' is 'b' and so on. Other codes signify the question numbers referred to.

Another popular cheating technique in multiple choice exams is 'lip-syncing' in which the examinee mouths the question number and answer to a nearby colleague. A little lip-reading practice beforehand has made this method quite successful for some students.

Other cheats are somewhat less sophisticated in their approach. They simply write their answers in large letters on smallish pieces of blank paper torn out of their answer booklets and hold them up for their friends to see while the supervisors have their backs turned. They do not seem to care if other students also catch their answers.

Moving furniture

Somebody's boring me—I think it's me.

Dylan Thomas

The role of examination supervisor could hardly be described as exciting, and at times it is all one can do to keep awake. Such was the case during a three-hour university chemistry exam when the sun came streaming into the examination room which was without sufficient protection on the windows. Conditions were far from comfortable for the students although none had complained.

The room was arranged so that the candidates were seated about 1.5 metres (five feet) apart. Each had a separate chair-cum-desk. They were required to write their answers in a booklet that rested on a flat arm that protruded from the chair frame itself. After about forty minutes without incident, the supervisor was fighting off sleep when something caught his eye.

Seated in the front row near the right-hand corner of the room was a female student wearing a green sweatshirt and matching shorts. At least, that was where the supervisor remembered her being at the start, and he was somewhat surprised to now see her sitting in a different position about halfway towards the back of the room. Since there had been no empty seats at the start of the exam, and assuming he had not been dreaming, then a switching of seats must have occurred while he wasn't looking.

Pretending not to notice anything amiss and to be looking the other way, he finally uncovered the truth. With imperceptible movements of her feet, the student was creeping with her chair toward that of another student. It took her nearly an hour to move about five metres.

The reason for the move became apparent when the culprit busied herself craning her neck to see what her new neighbour had written on his paper. The now alert supervisor simply walked to her chair and made a polite request that she steer herself in the direction of his own desk at the front of the room and complete the remainder of the exam right under his nose. Realising that her game was up, she immediately conceded defeat and was in place within about five seconds. No further action was taken.

EXCUSES FOR ALL OCCASIONS

Snoring sisters   Hungry snails

Phoney illnesses and injuries   Innocent parents

Caught in the rain   Blame the lecturer

Sleeping pills

Over-enthusiasm   Finding religion

Misreading the exam time

Developing a phobia

Friendly mechanics   Perspiration problems

Dietary blues

Drink-driving   Irresponsibility of others

Death in the family

Fear of failure   Dread of exams

Computer predicaments

Speeding trains

Blissful ignorance

Weighty issues

Transport difficulties

Wandering spouses

Acting the goat

Power blackouts   Fear of pencils

Clumsy parents

Blame the supervisor   Disappearing cats

Bomb scares   Keeping clean

Losing concentration   Exaggerated pains

Worries of the world ·   Multiple ailments

Unkind boyfriends   Conflicting lies

Sisterly love

Laugh and the world laughs with you, snore and you sleep alone.
Anthony Burgess, Inside Mr Enderby, *1968*

With breathtaking modesty, Pamela described herself as a 'sensible student' who was suffering great difficulties in her home life which warranted the special consideration of examiners. It transpired that, due to unforeseen circumstances, she was 'forced by her parents' to share a bedroom with her sister.

This was not expected to be a problem, but Pamela explained that it was a complete disaster as her sister had an inclination to snore and insisted on playing the radio at odd hours during the night. It was not revealed precisely what the sister endured at the hands of Pamela.

With refreshing abandon she declared that no human being should suffer as she now did. Unfortunately, she could not predict a change in her surroundings in the immediate future and, indeed, she hinted that her sister deliberately set out to annoy her as much as possible, although there was no evidence for this assertion.

Since her performance in recent exams had been a confirmation of a dismal showing in previous years, Pamela's request for leniency on 'human rights' grounds was dismissed by the university. It did, however, suggest she receive free counselling to attempt to alleviate her conditions, but she flatly refused to be involved.

Beware of garden pests

A tale never loses in the telling.

Proverb

Animals can play an important role in helping students avoid exams, although the old standby of 'the dog ate my homework' has lost its magic nowadays and more original ideas are called for.

Richard was an inventive first year student faced with the problem of how to avoid his upcoming make-up biology exam. He had already side-stepped the normal scheduled

exam with the help of a one-day medical certificate. It wasn't long before he hit on the idea of claiming complete ignorance of exactly when the make-up exam was to be held.

When the time came to make excuses, he simply said that he hadn't received the exam timetable in the mail and therefore did not know when and where to present himself. By the time he had made personal enquiries he was surprised to learn that the exam had already taken place. The authorities were emphatic that the information had been mailed out and were in the process of awarding him a failing grade.

Richard's future glory was assured when the following day he produced a wad of shredded paper. Announcing that it had been found at the bottom of his mailbox several weeks earlier, he admitted that his suspicions that it probably had been a letter in its previous life were now confirmed.

Richard's contention was that the missing letter containing the exam information apparently had been eaten by a particularly voracious group of snails that attacked his mail from time to time. This letter had apparently been the victim of a particularly savage attack such that it was now completely unrecognisable.

Oddly enough, Richard was given the benefit of the doubt by an appeals committee. Luckily for Richard, a committee member had also suffered a similar encounter with letter-eating snails.

Never say die

If at first you don't succeed, try, try again. Then quit. No use being a damn fool about it.

W.C. Fields (attrib.)

Appearances can be deceiving as evidenced by Gillian, a well-known malingerer in a business course. It was obvious to those who had dealt with her that she was capable of going to great lengths to avoid putting in any effort whatsoever.

On one occasion she appeared at the enquiry counter of the faculty with her head swathed in transparently false and ill-fitting bandages. Between moans, Gillian endeavoured to explain to the newly appointed secretary that she had fallen and hit her head resulting in 'severe injuries', and was totally unfit to sit for her final exam that day. To make matters worse, she did not 'have the strength' to seek medical attention. She requested that the secretary kindly bear witness to her plight and pass the message on to her lecturer.

The subterfuge may well have succeeded, except that one of her previous tutors happened to be passing. Witnessing the performance, the tutor remarked that this was an even more unconvincing effort than Gillian's last attempt at a similar deception.

With an engaging smile, Gillian began unravelling the bandages and, to the secretary's surprise, her head appeared quite normal. With a resigned shrug of the shoulders, the aspiring actor disappeared down the corridor toward the exam room calling out over her shoulder that 'it was worth a try'. The bewildered secretary could only stare in amazement while the tutor chuckled.

Always tell your mother

I never know how much of what I say is true.

Bette Midler

Physical injuries can indeed be debilitating and it is not unusual for them to be used as an excuse for a poor performance or even non-appearance at an exam.

In one such case, a small college received a letter from Therese, an enterprising statistics student, claiming that she had broken her writing arm and was unable to satisfactorily undertake her exam as scheduled. Could she please do it six weeks later when she would be in better shape?

The request seemed plausible enough and Therese's sympathetic tutor even rang her home to make special arrangements for a supplementary exam at a later date. Since he felt that she probably had enough problems, he decided not to worry about obtaining a medical certificate to verify her condition.

Unfortunately, Therese forgot to let her unsuspecting mother in on the deception and she unwittingly caused her daughter's downfall. Mum truthfully explained that Therese was unable to come to the phone since she was out playing a vigorous game of basketball in her weekly competition. She was quite bewildered when asked how her daughter's arm was progressing as she was unaware of any problem with it.

It came as no surprise to Therese when the university discipline committee made its judgement. It was a six months suspension in the sin-bin.

Singing in the rain

I must get out of these wet clothes and into a dry Martini.

Alexander Woolcott

Feeling refreshed is always important when undertaking a stressful examination. Kurt was one student who took this to the extreme when, on the day before his economics paper, he noticed that it was pouring with rain. He decided to go for a walk to clear his thoughts.

His written explanation was as follows.

> Since my clothing was apparently inadequate for the rain, I became soaked to the skin and this resulted in my becoming drowsy and having a very congested head. My condition became considerably worse and my doctor now advises that I need rest to regain my lost energy and not to do any exams for a while. Looking back it probably wasn't a smart thing to do.

Indeed it wasn't, since Kurt was already viewed by authorities as a disaster looking for somewhere to happen. Since it was considered that his predicament was self-inflicted, his request for deferment of the exam was denied. However, as badly as he apparently felt, he still managed to scrape a marginal pass.

Better late than never

Self praise is no recommendation.

Proverb

The telephone rang just before closing time in the examinations section of a large university. An unfortunate clerk soon found himself engaged in a remarkable conversation with an ex-student identifying herself as Ina. The caller explained firmly that she had graduated some ten years earlier and wished to speak to someone with regard to righting an injustice. It was clearly not a social call.

Ina explained that during her period at the university she had undertaken a course in introductory accounting that she managed to fail. However, after years of reflection, it was now clear to her that her failure was not due to any lack of ability on her part, but was caused by an appallingly uninspiring performance by the lecturer. It came to light that Ina was now in a middle-management position in a finance company and that the stigma of her failure had haunted her all this time. She certainly had no doubt about her capabilities. However, word of her past inadequacy had recently reached the ears of junior staff and she strongly suspected that there were whispers in the corridors about her apparent deficiencies.

Ina was amazed that she hadn't come to the realisation sooner that her disaster had been someone else's fault all along. However, this could now easily be rectified. Ina made a formal request that the fail grade be removed from her record so that she could 'get on with her life'. In addition, she demanded a fresh academic transcript with any mention of the offending accounting course removed.

The beleaguered clerk politely explained that this was indeed an unusual request and that if Ina wanted to apply for special consideration, then she was over nine years too late. Since all traces of her performance had long since been destroyed and her lecturer had unfortunately passed away, there was absolutely no chance of a grade reversal and Ina's record would remain intact.

The clerk's ears were still ringing several minutes later following Ina's ensuing verbal assault and slamming down of the phone.

Eight hours is not enough

What he lacks in intelligence, he makes up for in stupidity.

Anon.

It is generally accepted that having sufficient sleep is vital if the brain is to be functioning at full capacity during the day. Not surprisingly, many students experience restless nights before an important exam and find themselves still wide awake at 3.00 a.m. with a 9.00 a.m. exam looming.

In a burst of inspiration, an enterprising business student named Zolton found a novel way to sidestep the problem. His request for special consideration of his poor exam performance involved a claim that, after retiring at 10.00 p.m., he suffered a bout of insomnia and repeatedly glanced at the clock every ten minutes or so. In a distressed state by 2.30 a.m., it occurred to him that there was still time for a refreshing nap if he could help things along by taking a handful of sleeping pills. Since he lived on his own, the perhaps predictable result was that he slept not only through his alarm but for most of the day.

Although Zolton claimed 'circumstances beyond his control as a result of the side-effects of medication,' the examiners were not particularly sympathetic and frankly found the whole episode difficult to believe. In view of his poor course work he was not given the opportunity to display his talents at a make-up exam.

Losing track of time

Three o'clock is always too late or too early for anything you want to do.

Jean-Paul Sartre

Jay was an enthusiastic psychology student who liked to plan ahead. He arrived bright and early at 1.00 p.m. for his 2.00 p.m. exam, doing so, he claimed, in case there was a difficulty with the traffic. Noticing that he had some time to spare, he thought that it would be opportune to spend a few minutes in the library brushing up on those last-minute details.

Unfortunately, Jay explained, he became totally engrossed in his library work and completely forgot all about the exam until nearly 3.00 p.m., by which time he predicted that he would not be allowed to enter the exam room. So he went home.

Confronting the examiner the following morning, Jay maintained that it would be unjust to punish him since he was obviously such a keen student, suggesting that this was a rare quality nowadays. Would it be possible for him to do a make-up exam at a later date, say, in two weeks time?

Apparently he was unable to find any witnesses who saw him in the library or even to provide any evidence that he came on campus at all. His story was not believed and he failed the subject.

Timing is everything

I have noticed that people who are late are often so much jollier than the people who have to wait for them.

Robertson Davies

Sometimes, students turn up for an exam on the wrong day—inevitably sometime after the scheduled exam date. These students seem unable to correctly read the exam timetable that is widely distributed several weeks before the event. Occasionally the degree of lateness is taken to the limit.

Jennifer and Carly were typical of such cases—they both turned up exactly two weeks after scheduled exam day. They were asked to explain how they could both independently make such a gross mistake. Didn't they talk to other students in the meantime who might have made mention of sitting for the paper?

Apparently not. The women explained that they were good friends who lived together and 'did not socialise much'. It appeared that Carly read the exam timetable, got the date wrong, and promptly passed the information on to Jennifer who did not bother to check herself.

To the surprise of many, their story was believed by the examiners. Despite the fact that Jennifer should have made her own enquiries and checked the exam date, the case was considered special and both were allowed to undertake a make-up exam that they managed to pass.

A religious experience

Keep a diary and one day it'll keep you.

Mae West

It's a testing time for everybody when an exam supervisor catches red-handed a student who is cheating. An unsettling case was presented by Noel, an impressive engineering student who was about to confront the university discipline committee which would largely decide his short-term academic career, if any.

Noel was not prepared to offer any excuse for his behaviour, but was able to write at great length on the reason he should be exonerated. He explained that since the unfortun-

ate incident he had 'found Christ', and had noted his church attendances in a small diary which he produced. He politely suggested to the committee that 'any further punishment on the part of the committee was quite unnecessary' since God would apparently now be dealing with the matter.

It appeared true that Noel, at least according to his diary, was now indeed spending most of his waking hours in a church. The committee took the view, however, that this newfound fervour was irrelevant to the matter at hand and discharged its duty by providing the culprit with a one year suspension to see what else he could find.

Beware of dangerous books

Hypochondria is the only disease I haven't got.

Graffito, New York, 1978

It is understandable that in any large group of individuals, such as a student body, there will be some who suffer from one or a variety of illnesses, injuries or even phobias. Not uncommon is a fear of failure (kakorraphiaphobia) which many of us experience in a minor way from time to time. Indeed, some students who have a genuine fear of undertaking exams in large rooms (agoraphobia) are allowed to sit for their papers in isolation, while other relevant apprehensions include a fear of writing (graphophobia) and a fear of schools (scholionophobia).

It was left to Matthew, an inventive sociology student, to impress everybody by outlining his 'bibliophobia' in a detailed letter submitted to the examiners after he had failed his final exam. He explained that his unfortunate affliction had made life very difficult indeed, since he was unable to enter a bookshop without becoming stressed and had extreme difficulties even opening a text. To make matters worse, he claimed that his fear of books made it impossible for him to go near the library and so severely curtailed his study activities.

It was considered curious that Matthew had not raised this as an issue during his previous two years at the college, since he claimed to have had the condition 'for some time now'. Despite several apparent contradictions in his lengthy request, it was recommended that he be sent for counselling before any decision could be made.

Next time, catch the bus

I just solved the parking problem. I bought a parked car.
Henny Youngman, US comedian

On some occasions a student will tell a tale of woe that seems quite reasonable and beyond question. For example, Indira was a third year biology student who explained that she had the misfortune to experience car trouble on the way to her exam, such that by the time she arrived it was too late to commence. Could she undertake the make-up exam in four weeks time?

Challenged to produce evidence, Indira enclosed a letter from an enthusiastic mechanic who clearly stated the time and date when he attended her broken-down car. It all fitted in nicely and the lecturer was on the verge of complying with Indira's request.

However, at the last minute, he made a routine check of Indira's records which contained all her previous university correspondence. The result was completely unexpected since it appeared, encouraged by former successes, that this was the third time she had used the same story. Moreover, all three letters had been written by the same mechanic.

In her increasing confidence, Indira had overplayed her hand. Not only was her request denied, but she was probably lucky to escape with only a warning not to attempt another such deception in the future.

Keep your cool

Genius is one per cent inspiration and ninety-nine per cent perspiration.
Thomas Edison, newspaper interview, 1911

The engineering exam had been in progress for about an hour with the class seemingly engrossed in a challenging paper. However, the attention of an observant supervisor was attracted by a student in the second row, as every few minutes he was engaged in vigorously rubbing his hands together and then wiping them on his jeans.

Her curiosity suitably aroused, she approached the perpetrator and asked him if everything was in order. Apparently it wasn't. Indeed, he declared that he was pleased that she had asked and was sufficiently concerned to notice his difficulties.

He confidently explained that he was a victim of circumstance, since his palms had chosen this inopportune occasion to sweat profusely and he was therefore unable to grip his pen properly. He put the attack down to an acute apprehension about his ability to pass the subject.

Warming to the task, he promptly requested an 'extra thirty minutes or so' to allow for this unfortunate affliction. Although the supervisor expressed appropriate sympathy for his plight, she regretted that it was not possible to oblige him and he was left with an abundance of perspiration but apparently little inspiration as he did not manage to pass.

Always have a six-pack handy

Food is an important part of a balanced diet.

Fran Lebowitz, Metropolitan Life, *1978*

As all students know, it is wise to keep your strength up before tackling a gruelling three-hour exam paper. You wouldn't get any argument on this issue from Anna, a diligent student who was prepared to spend long hours in the library.

Unfortunately, Anna found her exam preparation was being severely hampered by 'the early closing of food outlets on campus'. To make matters worse, on those occasions when sustenance was available she found it to be 'inedible' since it contained too much sugar, fat or cholesterol. Moreover, she declared there was a 'distinct lack of variety and quality in the available snacks'. What was this gifted student to do when she required refreshment?

Due to these intolerable (and possibly life-threatening) circumstances, Anna requested that her complaint be considered when marking her exam paper.

It apparently had not occurred to her to bring her own food.

Drink-driving doesn't pay

One reason I don't drink is that I want to know if I'm having a good time.

Nancy Astor

Trevor explained that his study routine was going well until the night before his final exam in accounting. It was then that his father learned that Trevor had lost his licence after being caught 'speeding and with a mid-range of alcohol'. Although Trevor had obviously been aware of the suspension for some time, the news came as a complete surprise to his unsuspecting parents.

Trevor made an impassioned plea to his examiners for special consideration of his sub-standard exam performance, claiming that parental displeasure had severely disrupted his study.

> Perhaps I should have told Dad earlier but it didn't seem like a good idea. It wouldn't have been so bad except that it was an important exam and it was plain bad luck that he found out right when he did. He went through the roof and spent the rest of the night ranting and raving so that I don't even remember getting any sleep at all.

Trevor insisted that his motive in not informing his father earlier of his transgression was to spare himself distress before the exams and to avoid a scene exactly like the one that occurred. However, his request for special consideration was not warmly received by the university as it was felt that he was a victim of his own making.

Unfortunately his troubles didn't end there, as for his driving offence Trevor earned a substantial fine and the opportunity to sample public transport for twelve months.

Never trust a friend

Your friend is the man who knows all about you, and still likes you.
Elbert Hubbard, The Notebook, *1927*

Sarah was set a history essay worth a large percentage of her final assessment. She was required to hand it in before the commencement of the three-week vacation. In a letter to the examiners she claimed to have completed the work well before time but, because of her busy schedule, 'gave it to a boyfriend to mail in'.

After assurances from the alleged boyfriend that he would carry out her request, Sarah went on holidays and was 'basically uncontactable', secure in the knowledge that her work would be submitted before the due date.

When the vacation was over, Sarah appeared at her lecturer's office with her essay nicely presented in a folder. Refreshingly untarnished by embarrassment, she explained it was unavoidably late and she really couldn't be blamed. Apparently she had been horrified to learn that her boyfriend had 'lost the university's address' and had made no effort whatsoever to locate it and lodge the essay. It was later revealed that the boyfriend in fact lived only about six blocks from the campus.

To compound Sarah's predicament, the pair had 'broken off their relationship' following a fight over the incident. The hapless Sarah expressed extreme surprise when it was announced that her essay would not be accepted since it was her responsibility to make sure her work was received on time. Presumably her former boyfriend is still wondering where the university is.

Death by misadventure

It's a funny old world—a man's lucky if he can get out of it alive.
W.C. Fields, You're Telling Me, *screenplay, 1934*

The death of a close family member is understandably a traumatic event and a deserved degree of sympathy is given by examiners. The passing of a distant relative who has resided overseas for a number of years, however, may be regarded with some scepticism when an attempt is made to use it to a student's advantage.

In some universities it is required that a copy of a death certificate or appropriate newspaper notice be provided as evidence of a death if special consideration for exams is requested. Usually this is accompanied by a letter from the student containing a brief outline of events. One university received three unusual letters in which students gave accounts of family tragedies. The following are direct quotations.

> Unfortunately my father died before he was cremated.

> I had to attend the funeral parlour that day. This was because my mother had died before the funeral.

> After my husband died I buried myself in my books.

Attempts to verify the accuracy of these assertions met with failure.

Gloomy outlook is not unusual

There is much to be said for failure. It is more interesting than success.

Max Beerbohm, Mainly on the Air, *1947*

Rochelle was a keen history student who apparently had experienced no difficulty with her work at high school, but found that the step up to university level was somewhat beyond her capabilities. Appreciating her own incompetence, she was aware that the path to second year was going to be blocked by her failure in the recently completed first year final examinations.

Within days of learning her dismal results, this fine student fired off a heart-wrenching story to her examiners explaining that her lack of success on this occasion had left her not only 'traumatised' but also 'extremely depressed'. In view of the fact that her failure had upset her so much, she boldly requested a make-up exam to render her the opportunity to 'get her life together again'.

As much as they like cheerful students, the appeals board explained it was not all that unusual for students to be despondent when their expectations were not met, and that Rochelle would have to find another way to beat the blues.

Mathematics can be a health hazard

I have a new philosophy. I'm only going to dread one day at a time.
Charles Schultz, Peanuts

It is no secret that mathematics can have an adverse effect on the best of people. A mathematics exam paper may even bring on a variety of ailments, even though the candidate may have felt fine before starting. Such was the case with Haryanto who diligently prepared himself for what he suspected would be a vigorous calculus exam.

When he received his failing grade, Haryanto provided the appeals committee with a lengthy description of how his physical condition deteriorated during the paper. It partly read:

> I felt okay to begin with but as time went on I knew something was wrong. At the end I was completely exhausted. That exam left me nauseous, lethargic, despondent, ill-prepared to cope and with a desire to leave the room as quickly as possible. Also, I had an inability to focus properly.

At a later interview he confessed that he usually had a 'dread of examinations' and, to be frank, mathematics had always been a particular problem. Since a great many people feel that way about mathematics, Haryanto's request to do a make-up paper was denied.

The writing is on the wall

To err is human, but to really foul things up requires a computer.

Anon.

The computer age is well and truly upon us and is apparently causing difficulties where none previously existed. Although computers are generally designed to make life easier, it was left to Lisa, a first year science student, to point out an unexpected problem. Several days before her geology exam she requested that she be allowed extra writing time because of her 'unique difficulties'.

Displaying an impressive lack of versatility, she explained:

> I have been using computers to do all my writing for the past ten years and am now incapable of normal handwriting. I can't even write a shopping list any more. The only exception is writing cheques. Could I please have extra time to do the exam paper to account for this distressing problem?

Her plea was considered an interesting variation on those tales of woe told by students who can't add 2 + 2 without having a calculator handy. Although creating a good deal of mirth for the examiners, Lisa's request was respectfully declined.

Shut the windows

Rail travel at high speed is not possible, because passengers, unable to breathe, would die of asphyxia.

Professor Dionysus Lardner, Irish scientific writer, c. 1830

In some exams students are allowed to bring in one or two sheets of paper containing formulae or other material that is difficult to memorise. To forget to bring these documents on exam day is a complete disaster and condemns the student to almost certain failure.

This is exactly what happened to Dave, a student in management who found himself ready to start the exam without his precious formula sheet. Undeterred, he sat for the paper with predictably dismal results.

Several days later, Dave wrote to the examiners and explained that he had not forgotten the necessity of taking his sheets to the exam, but, rather, with a heartening efficiency, had placed them on the car seat next to him as he drove to the university. Unfortunately, he had forgotten to close the car window and a freak gust of wind 'sucked the notes out of the window and onto nearby railway tracks where they were run over by a passing train which appeared to be speeding'.

Naturally his notes seemed irretrievable and he was not prepared to risk his life to find them. He suggested that his poor exam performance was therefore quite understandable. Since there was no evidence of Dave's mishap and his class work was well below standard, the examiners did not see things his way.

Two for the price of one

Things are not always what they seem.

Proverb

Justin would certainly be the first to admit that he wasn't a star mathematics student. In fact, his work was so poor in his first year calculus course that he had seriously contemplated not even bothering to turn up for the final exam.

However, displaying uncharacteristic bravado, he prepared himself to sit for the gruelling three-hour paper. Upon taking his seat and flipping through the questions during reading time, he was taken aback by the fact that he appeared to have been given two distinct exam papers, one stapled to the back of the other. The top one was the calculus paper he had expected but, curiously, the one underneath was a three-hour paper on algebra clearly intended for students in a higher level subject because the questions made little sense to him. As it happened, the algebra paper had been attached in error by an examination official and Justin was the only student in the exam room to receive a double helping of questions.

Brushing aside any lingering doubts about the situation, Justin soon decided that the second paper was a bonus for *all* students to pick up extra marks and that there was nothing particularly amiss. He proceeded to do his best in both exams. Working feverishly, he completed as many questions as he could in the three hours. Unfortunately, these turned out to be depressingly few.

In a later interview. Justin admitted that he was a little puzzled at finding six hours' worth of exam questions on his desk, and had found both papers equally difficult. It did not occur to him to question this oddity and he simply assumed that everyone else was in the same situation.

In view of their mistake, the examiners allowed Justin to sit for a fresh paper several days later. Unfortunately, these results weren't any better than his first efforts.

A weighty problem

When I go to the beauty parlour I always use the emergency entrance. Sometimes I just go for an estimate.

Phyllis Diller

New heights of mastery in excuses were reached by Heidi, an average ability occupational therapy student who had apparently found the recent semester somewhat difficult. Matters were not helped by the acquisition of a new boyfriend who seemed to occupy her time when she should have been attending class.

With a poor performance imminent in the final exam, which would result in her possibly having to repeat the year, Heidi decided to beat the administration to the punch before even attempting her exams. She inscribed a detailed letter explaining that, regretfully, life was not running smoothly owing to 'personal difficulties'. In particular, she referred to a 'ballooning weight' problem.

She revealed that the recent deterioration of her physical appearance had not escaped her attention but, initially, had caused her no problem. The real difficulty was with her boyfriend who apparently felt the need to emphasise her excessive weight at every opportunity. In an attempt to please him, Heidi had gone on a crash diet that had left her 'weak and unable to focus properly'. As a result, a possibly poor performance in her upcoming exams must be viewed with this in mind.

Unfortunately, her attempts were doomed to failure since her achievements in the paper were so far below satisfactory that even a poor diet could not excuse them. Officials refrained from advising her to get a new boyfriend.

Transport blues

I don't want money. It is only people who pay their bills who want that, and I never pay mine.

Oscar Wilde, The Picture of Dorian Gray, *1891*

An adventurous chemistry student, Eddie revealed to friends that he was determined to escape the rigours of his upcoming examination. Since he was in a particularly fine state of health, he decided that there was little point in attempting the subterfuge of a trumped-up medical ailment. Besides, he had tried that twice before. It was therefore necessary to engage an alternative course of action.

On this occasion the grand scheme involved an effort to play on the sympathy of the examiners. After failing to turn up on the day of the exam, Eddie penned an impressive thesis to the authorities on how difficult life had been owing to a severe shortage of finances during the semester. So bad were his circumstances, that on the morning of the paper he found himself completely devoid of funds. He did not even have the money to pay the bus fare to the university.

He explained that the only way for him to get to the exam was to stand on the corner of a busy highway and hitchhike. It was not his fault that nobody was prepared to stop, and after an hour or so he gave up and simply went home and wrote his letter. He added that 'being poor is not a crime' and emphasised that it would be most unjust to penalise him since he did his best to attend. These were clearly circumstances beyond his control.

However, when asked to produce some evidence of his assertions, Eddie was unable to provide any witnesses to his hitchhiking attempt or evidence that a bus fare was out of reach. He was failed for non-attendance without an acceptable explanation.

Wandering spouses

Thou shalt not commit adultery . . . unless in the mood.

W.C. Fields

The college career of Brenda was the subject of interruption throughout its three year history. For the first twelve months she was continually submitting special consideration requests for examinations along the lines that she lived so far from campus that she had to spend a ridiculous amount of time travelling each day by public transport. This resulted in her arriving home in the evenings so late that she was too tired to cook any dinner and went straight to bed.

To make matters worse, she had to leave home so early in the morning that there was no time for breakfast. This left only a brief period in the middle of the day for a snack that substituted for lunch as she did not have the funds available to purchase a decent meal. As a result, Brenda had lost considerable weight and continually 'felt faint'.

Brushing aside suggestions to seek medical advice, counselling or to consider moving closer to the college, Brenda, in her second year of studies, reached new heights when she wrote and explained that she had been married in the long vacation. However, her position had not improved, but worsened as her new husband had developed the habit of bringing his girlfriends home. The reasons for this were not entirely clear, although Brenda's life had become even more miserable.

On the first occasion that the husband's indiscretions were raised in her submission for special consideration, they evoked substantial sympathy from the staff and Brenda's marginal performances were treated with leniency. However, during the next twelve months, Brenda consistently forwarded similar requests to the examiners, with the minor variation that apparently she had cooled relations with her spouse to the extent that she did not care so much anymore about him bringing his girlfriends home. The real problem seemed to be that this habit of her husband disrupted her valuable study time as she was required to 'tend to their needs' during visits.

After about six such submissions the college had heard enough, and deepest sympathies for her unfortunate situation were conveyed by all concerned. However, Brenda was informed that the time had come to rearrange her personal life and that she could no longer expect special consideration in every exam for which she sat.

It was agreed that Brenda could defer her studies for twelve months and then gain automatic readmission to the college if her circumstances improved. Although she readily agreed to these terms, Brenda never reappeared.

Don't act the goat

I do not like animals. Of any sort. I don't even like the idea of animals. Animals are no friends of mine. They occupy no space in my heart. Animals are off my list.

Fran Lebowitz, Social Studies, *1981*

Some excuses are so lengthy that they take on the form of a short novel. One engaging narrative was presented by Shane, a student of philosophy who revealed that his parents had recently purchased a small goat farm just out of the city.

The grazing area was apparently so thick with undergrowth that the unfortunate animals constantly found themselves covered in annoying burrs. After a lengthy description of the hazards of bringing up goats, Shane lamented that his valuable time was frequently disrupted by his parents' demands that he remove the offending burrs.

He requested special consideration of his poor exam performance as the burr-removing exercise 'consumed most of his waking hours when he would normally be studying'. The examiner found it hard to believe that Shane was serious but apparently he was, since brief enquiries confirmed a farm full of goats at Shane's address.

However, it was explained to Shane that his obligation to undertake farm chores at home was a family matter and did not fall within the guidelines specified for 'misadventure'.

Don't wake me if I'm asleep

I have picked up a pretty sound working knowledge of electrical matters. It is not comprehensive, God knows—I still can't fully understand why you can't boil an egg on an electric guitar . . .

Keith Waterhouse, The Passing of the Third-floor Buck, *1974*

Catriona was an engaging student who had not shown much enthusiasm for politics throughout the course and it was widely suspected that she had only enrolled because one of her boyfriends had done so. It was therefore not a complete surprise when she missed the final examination, although several days later she set a high standard in special consideration requests.

The final examination was scheduled to be held on a Monday morning and Catriona had been 'busy studying all Sunday afternoon'—at least from 3.00 p.m. onwards. The lecturer privately held the view that this was most likely the sum total of her study for the duration of the three month course.

Preparing to lay it on thick with a lengthy description, Catriona explained that around 5.00 p.m. there was an electricity failure in her street and, being the middle of winter, the house was suddenly plunged into darkness. She suspected that the blackout would only be brief so she welcomed the opportunity to lie down on her bed for a few minutes until power was restored. With due modesty, she declared that her prediction was quite accurate, since the total length of the blackout was only about fifteen minutes.

All would have been well, except that poor Catriona fell asleep and nobody bothered to wake her. At least not until 8.00 a.m. the next day. The realisation that all her study time had evaporated led to a 'panic attack' and she was in no shape to confront a gruelling three-hour paper on political issues. So she stayed at home and wrote to the examiners.

Catriona requested a make-up exam on the grounds that electricity problems were beyond her control and went on to pile blame on her hapless parents who should have known better than to let her lie asleep all night. Apparently they had felt that the extra rest would do her good.

Unfortunately, the lecturer concluded that Catriona's excuse, although original, was unconvincing and her request was denied.

Keep a pen handy

You go to a psychiatrist when you're slightly cracked and keep going until you're completely broke.

Anon.

Dewi was a geology student destined for a brilliant career. Unfortunately, it wasn't going to be in geology. It was not entirely clear when her trouble first surfaced, she explained on the eve of her final exam, but it was definitely going to be a handicap. A large portion of the geology exam paper consisted of multiple choice questions that were going to be marked using an optical scanner. One requirement was that the answer forms be filled in using pencil. And that was the cause of Dewi's anxiety.

For reasons probably best left unknown, Dewi had developed a 'pencil phobia'. That is, whenever she was required to use (or apparently even go near) a pencil she broke out with sweaty palms, a nasty neck rash and acute distress. This made undertaking such an exam impossible and she made a request to be graded solely on her course work. This consisted of a few assignments which the examiners suspected had being done in conjunction with a few friends.

Impressively, Dewi provided documents from a psychiatrist which explained that she was being treated for 'an ongoing condition'. However, no mention of pencils was made.

Dewi was informed by the examiners that her disheartening state of affairs could be easily overcome. Dewi would be given a special dispensation so that she could fill in the answer sheet using a pen. Her answer sheet would then be hand marked (by a human) so that the optical scanner would not be offended.

Surprisingly, when this solution was presented to Dewi she did not take it well. Although pens did not cause a particular problem, the whole episode had traumatised her to the extent that she had become increasingly nervous at the prospect of sitting for any type of exam. However, given the circumstances she did so, and it is pleasing to report that both Dewi and the pen did sufficiently well to gain a low-grade pass.

Parents clean up

The only reason I always try to meet and know the parents better is because it helps me forgive their children.

Louis Jabannot

Con was painfully aware that his major essay on marketing principles was due no later than 10.00 a.m. the next morning and non-submission would spell certain failure. He was also mindful that since it was nearly midnight he had no chance of meeting the deadline for a project he hadn't even begun. Extraordinary measures were called for, and, in a flash of brilliance, he created a fanciful tale of woe that he felt sure would gain him an extension of time.

In his letter of explanation, Con related that he had spent many fruitful hours researching the topic and had only to give his essay the odd finishing touch here and there for it to be a really first-class effort. However, he had made the dreadful mistake of leaving his only copy lying on the coffee table in the lounge room.

Regrettably, while Con was attending classes at college, his younger brother had knocked a cup of tea all over his masterpiece. His mother had come rushing in to discover a 'gooey mess' and had promptly put it in the waste-paper bin. Such was its state, she had mistaken it for scrap. The next night, Con's father emptied the bin into the rest of the garbage which was collected the following morning.

Con was completely unaware of this disastrous chain of events until he frantically tried to locate the missing essay. His parents were grief-stricken at the pain they had caused Con since there was certainly no chance of now retrieving the essay. Moreover, Con confessed that he had destroyed all the notes relating to his efforts since he had felt it was basically complete. However, given a further few weeks, he felt sure that he could submit an equally fine piece of work.

In a cunning manoeuvre, and without warning the unfortunate student, the lecturer rang Con's home and spoke to both his mother and father for verification of the incident. Overcome with embarrassment, they had to admit that it all came as a complete surprise to them.

At a subsequent meeting of the discipline committee, Con admitted that his half-baked scheme had backfired badly and that he was now having 'severe family difficulties'. Sensing he didn't need any further trouble, the members decided not to suspend him but simply awarded a mark of zero for the essay along with a stern warning. Con went on to fail marketing and changed his major to psychology.

It wasn't my fault

I love mankind—it's people I can't stand.

Charles Schultz, Peanuts

It is widely suggested that some students perform badly in examinations not because of ignorance but owing to poor technique. High accolades must go to Yee who managed to defend both her knowledge and her methodology and still find the reason for her abysmal performance in a business communication exam. She blamed the supervisors.

In a sustained attack, the aggrieved student let forth with a written barrage of criticism that made the exam conditions sound worse than a war zone. It was therefore curious that no other student had registered any criticisms.

To begin, Yee complained that the supervisors were 'far too old' for such an undertaking and were clearly 'out of touch with the feelings of young students like myself'. Specific difficulties regarding age were not elaborated upon, although similar comments had been made on previous occasions by other students.

In detailing alleged incidents, Yee claimed that one female supervisor wore high heels that annoyingly 'clicked like a horse' as she paced up and down the aisle, while a male supervisor repeatedly stopped to 'glance over my shoulder at what I was writing'. This had made her 'tense and anxious'.

To make matters worse, one of the elderly female supervisors had fallen asleep on her strategically placed chair near the door and was twitching to such an extent that Yee felt she could have been having a heart attack. She also claimed that two whispering supervisors repeatedly broke her concentration by outlining their previous weekend's activities.

It was claimed that the combination of these appalling incidents resulted in her outstandingly awful exam paper. Although the supervisors vigorously denied any of the outlined circumstances, on the strength of good classwork Yee was awarded a make-up exam which she undertook with a lone, young examiner sitting silently in the front of the room. Interestingly, she performed extremely well.

A cat-astrophe strikes

A man was attacked and left bleeding in a ditch. Two sociologists passed by and one said to the other: 'We must find the person who did this—they need help'.

Anon.

Barbara had been admitted to the sociology program at university and her lecturers were in no doubt that she was making an all-out effort to do well. It was unfortunate that she appeared to be overwhelmed by family matters. These invariably involved some crazy scheme on the part of her husband, Jim, or the unruly antics of their seemingly uncontrollable three-year-old son.

Nevertheless, there was every expectation that she would ultimately pass the course with reasonable ease. The lecturer was therefore understandably dismayed when Barbara failed to turn up for the final exam and did not submit any reason for doing so. In a touching but unusual gesture, he rang her at home to check that everything was in order and to hopefully obtain an explanation for her absence.

With a faltering voice, Barbara related an extraordinary incident that occurred on the morning of the exam. As she was driving out of her garage to come to the university, she noticed that her cat was sitting on a branch very high up in a tree in her front yard. She had never seen him at such a height before so she stopped the engine and summoned her husband.

Jim came to the hasty conclusion that the cat was indeed stuck, but made immediate plans to climb the tree and undertake a rescue. He assured Barbara that the whole process would only occupy five minutes or so but asked her to wait to make sure he didn't fall.

Predictably, Jim himself became wedged in the tree, replacing the cat who had apparently found no difficulty in coming back down to earth. Barbara called the fire brigade who managed to retrieve a somewhat chastened Jim from his lofty position, but by that time it was far too late for Barbara to attend the exam.

She had not reported the incident to the university as she felt sure that nobody would believe her. She was greatly relieved when not only did the examiners do so, but were not even surprised, given their knowledge of Jim. Barbara was allowed to sit for a make-up exam that she passed with flying colours.

Problems even out

Several excuses are always less convincing than one.

Aldous Huxley, Point Counter Point, *1928*

English was such a popular subject at a particular university that it was not possible to seat all of the candidates for the final examination in the one place. However, there were two large rooms (A and B) available for the exam, on the opposite side of the campus to each other.

To facilitate matters, students were divided into two groups of roughly equal size which were randomly assigned to either room A or B. This was not an uncommon practice with large enrolments and had not presented any real difficulty to date. The same exam paper was given in each room at the same time.

This particular exam was a three-hour paper and matters proceeded smoothly for the first hour or so. Then an anonymous phone call was received at the administration office declaring that a bomb had been planted in building A and was timed to detonate in thirty minutes. An attendant was dispatched to the building in question and whispered the unpleasant news to the two supervisors.

According to regulations, the students were instructed to cease writing immediately and leave the room, and the building, in an orderly fashion and to assemble in a grassy area some distance away. Unfortunately, nobody told the students that they couldn't have a chat along the way. Not surprisingly, many had a lengthy conversation about the exam paper during the forty minute wait while the room was searched.

When the crisis was finally declared a hoax, the students were led back into the room and given appropriate extra time to complete the paper. Not surprisingly, the examination centre was subsequently besieged with special consideration requests from poorly performing students. These included students in room A who were either upset by the bomb scare or distressed at seeing some of their fellow students discussing the exam paper when they themselves claimed not to have done so. Students from room B were indignant that they hadn't the same opportunity as those in room A to discuss the exam paper.

The administration was left with a giant mess. Interestingly, statistical analysis revealed no significant difference between the overall marks of the students in the two rooms. Armed with this information, the university decided that things had probably 'evened themselves out' and decided against holding another exam. Students received the grades they were originally awarded and all consideration requests were denied.

Dangerous showers

I don't like baths. I don't enjoy them in the slightest and, if I could, I'd prefer to go around dirty.

J. B. Priestley, Observer, *1979*

Marcus provided great entertainment when he submitted his reason for an uncharacteristically low score in his chemistry exam. In his own words, he had become engaged in a 'fight with the shower' that morning and had come off second best.

Being somewhat intrigued, his lecturer requested further details before any consideration could be given. Marcus explained that he had arisen bright and early on the morning of the exam so that he might snatch a few extra minutes of cramming. In order to refresh himself, he planned to give his hair a 'vigorous wash to clear my head'.

In his over-enthusiasm, his eyes became 'full of shampoo' and he became 'disoriented'. This resulted in him slipping on a cake of soap, at which point he wildly lashed out and grabbed at anything he could. This turned out to be the shower-head which came off in his hand. The resulting torrent of water sent him headlong into the glass screen where he 'bashed his head', but at least the shampoo had been washed out of his eyes.

By the time he managed to stem the flood, take some headache pills and have a brief lie-down, all of his study time had evaporated and he felt totally exhausted. Hence his poor exam performance.

Marcus was relieved to gain the sympathy of the entire department and was allowed to sit for a make-up exam that he passed.

Keep your mind on the job

My son has taken up meditation—at least it's better than sitting doing nothing.

Max Kauffman

It had been a tough morning, as Sol explained in an appeal against his fail grade in a history exam. The day got off to a fine start when he awoke and prepared himself to drive to college for the 9.00 a.m. paper. It was around 7.45 a.m., during his customary relaxing bath in which he was fond of meditating, that Sol evidently 'lost my concentration'. This resulted in severe difficulties, including a failure to remember exactly what he had to pack in his bag. Several important items, such as his textbook and lunch, were forgotten.

Sol's lack of confidence reached new depths when he found himself driving along the highway, still 'without my concentration'. This resulted in his proceeding through a give-way sign and sideswiping another car that had the right of way. After a brief exchange of licence details, Sol continued his journey and finally made it to the examination room. Sadly, his concentration still eluded him since he found himself staring at an exam paper which he had no idea how to begin.

He bemoaned the fact that no matter how hard he tried, 'my concentration would not come back to me'. This resulted in a virtually blank answer book after three hours of effort.

With a deep sense of gratitude, Sol was awarded a make-up exam two weeks later but was unable to improve significantly on his first effort. His concentration had deserted him yet again.

Tummy trouble

Never drink black coffee at lunch; it will keep you awake in the afternoon.

Jilly Cooper, How to Survive from Nine to Five, *1970*

Transcending conventional grammar, an inspiring plea by a first year philosophy student was hopelessly dreadful in its presentation. Nikki began her letter by announcing that the day before the examination she awoke feeling 'pretty sick'. So much so, apparently, that she 'forgot to eat for about twenty hours'. After realising the error of her ways, she decided to drink some coffee 'in order to acquire some energy'.

The exact quantity of coffee consumed remains a mystery, but some thirty minutes afterwards Nikki 'felt as if I had been poisoned'. The symptoms were stomachache, headache, dizziness, diarrhoea and 'loss of direction'. She continued in this state until late in the evening when a visit to an emergency medical centre confirmed that she was indeed unwell, but perhaps not as ill as she suggested to the examiners.

Nevertheless, against medical advice, Nikki thought she would 'give the exam a go' the next morning as 'I thought it had all gone away'. Much to her consternation, it hadn't. Right on cue, after about twenty minutes of floundering with an essay, she alleged that she developed a 'serious headache' and felt 'clammy'.

Her answers were a complete disaster and it was no real surprise that she comfortably managed to fail. In view of the available evidence, it was widely suspected that a mild stomach upset had been magnified into a major medical emergency. However, Nikki's literary efforts paid off and she was allowed to undertake a make-up exam that earned her a conceded pass.

EXCUSES FOR ALL OCCASIONS   71

Worries of the world

He's turned life around. He used to be depressed and miserable. Now he's miserable and depressed.

David Frost, TVAM, 1984

The not entirely promising career of Brendan, an arts student who had displayed a considerable lack of talent throughout his brief college career, did not get off to a good start when he achieved predictable fail grades in every exam.

With refreshing enthusiasm, however, this keen scholar submitted special consideration letters to each of his lecturers. The common theme was that his poor performance was due to 'severe depression'. Considering his non-existent academic ability this might have been understandable, but it seemed that Brendan was upset about a multitude of world events, and each examiner was subjected to a different tale of woe.

For example, the philosophy lecturer received a treatise on how disturbing it was that there appeared to be a hole in the ozone layer that would ultimately result in 'the imminent demise of mankind as we know it'. The history department was told that the war in Bosnia 'would probably never end', and even if it did there would always be another conflict to take its place somewhere else. The anthropology examiners did not escape the gloom when they were made aware of all the hunger and suffering in the world, while the psychologists were reminded that 'crime is everywhere' and that 'nobody is safe'.

In view of these constant worries, Brendan requested that he be allowed to undertake make-up examinations, the granting of which, he hinted, would cheer him up considerably. The alleged burning intensity of his emotions on world issues came as somewhat of a surprise to the administration since Brendan had always outwardly appeared to be a high-spirited individual.

Before making any firm recommendation, it was decided that several sessions with a university counsellor would uncover the truth of the matter. Indeed they did, since Brendan soon admitted that the whole letter-writing episode was a stunt suggested by a friend who had experienced limited success with a similar effort at another college.

The plan was doomed to failure when Brendan overplayed his hand. The astonishing variety of depressing events cited, combined with a lacklustre performance throughout the courses gave rise to justifiable suspicion. Brendan decided to 'give college a miss' for a couple of years after which he vowed to return and 'try his hand again'.

A medical miracle

Between two evils I always pick the one I never tried before.
Mae West, Klondike Annie, *screenplay*, *1936*

Maria had a burning desire to become an accountant and was quite prepared to undertake whatever means were necessary to achieve her goal. Unfortunately, her student career was sinking fast since, after a promising start in first year, she found herself quite unable to cope with the rigours of second year business law or come to grips with various accounting systems. The upcoming end of year examinations were threatening to be a nightmare and she was convinced that her only chance of passing all of them was to delay one until a later date. This necessitated a request for special consideration.

Maria considered two options. One was to visit an 'understanding' doctor, pretend to feel ill and get a medical certificate, while the other was to make up a colourful excuse. Since she had successfully tried the medical scam at the two previous exam periods, her best option was to come up with a convincing story.

After failing to make an appearance at the regular business law exam, Maria submitted a cry for help in the form of a lengthy thesis on both her personal and physical problems. To begin, she alluded to her 'ongoing hypertension problem', although there was no supporting evidence of this, and followed up with a variety of psychological ailments including 'mental stress which causes my heart to flutter' and 'anguish brought on by apprehension of the examinations'. Other problems included 'clammy perspiration' along with 'persistent dull pains in the chest'.

Warming to the task, her letter went on to describe in graphic detail a bout of food poisoning, probably due to a hearty meal of 'oily fish and chips'. Space does not permit a complete list of the alleged misfortunes suffered, but almost any one of them would have been sufficient to gain the required sympathy.

Although Maria was awarded a make-up exam, her efforts were in vain since she not only failed to pass that paper, but was unsuccessful in her final economics exam as well. She was last seen contemplating her career choice.

Too many boyfriends

We only confess our little faults to persuade people that we don't have any large ones.

Duc de la Rochefoucauld

Charlotte was a mediocre student of the classics, but one who had a special place in the hearts of the lecturers with her engaging personality and determination to work to the best of her ability. It was beyond the comprehension of even her close friends why she chose to dote on her boyfriend, Brett, since it was quite plain that he did not return her affection. Indeed, most found him quite an obnoxious individual who appeared to take pleasure in Charlotte's misery and often treated her with almost callous disregard.

It so happened that several weeks before the final examination, Brett found himself another student girlfriend and made no bones about dumping the apparently grief-stricken Charlotte. She seemed genuinely depressed and informed everyone, including staff, that the distraction of seeing her former partner around the campus with a new companion would have a detrimental effect on her exam performance.

To emphasise her distress, Charlotte poured her heart out in a letter to the examiners, requesting that, though she understood that personal problems were not usually considered a misadventure, perhaps her anguish could be taken into account. The scheme may well have worked except that a linguistics lecturer had seen her a couple of weeks before holding hands and cuddling someone who was obviously not Brett in a shopping centre.

Called into the office to expand upon her request, Charlotte was casually asked about the recent sighting of a new man in her life. She blushed and modestly confessed that she hadn't exactly lied in her letter, but had merely embellished the truth a little to gain some sympathy. The facts were that she had 'gone off' Brett a couple of months previously and his 'breaking it off' was a blessing in disguise. Apparently her new attachment was a significant improvement in all departments and was the real reason why her study time had recently been curtailed.

Although her plea for consideration was denied on this occasion, it appeared that the latest romance did have a positive influence since her subsequent grades were the best she had ever achieved.

A liar needs a good memory

Truth is a rare and precious commodity. We must be sparing in its use.

C.P. Scott, Spectator, *1982*

Keeping track of your stories is a necessity if you're in the business of fabricating excuses. Unfortunately for Herman, his memory was so poor that his efforts were merely laughable.

His troubles began when he made the decision not to sit for the final examination in accounting. He thought it would be simple to contrive a little excuse to explain away his absence. Exhibiting a deal of confidence, he made an arrangement with his girlfriend, Glenda, to write a letter on his behalf, saying that he was 'too ill to attend the exam that day as a result of chest pains'. Moreover, he did not feel well enough to get out of bed to visit a doctor, but much to his delight and surprise he recovered fully the next day.

Glenda was dispatched to hand-deliver the letter to the university, where authorities noted the lack of medical evidence along with the fact that Herman had not actually signed the letter himself. Glenda was asked to take the letter back to her boyfriend for his signature attesting to the outlined version of events.

When there was no correspondence forthcoming for a week, an official rang Herman and, without mentioning the visit from Glenda, asked him why he had not attended his accounting exam. The response was that he was 'overseas on urgent work-related business on that day and it was impossible to return to Australia in time'. He made no mention of any illness. Without wishing to alert him, the official asked Herman to put these facts in an affidavit 'for the records'. Herman said this would not be a problem.

Two days later the legal document was delivered to the university. In it, Herman stated that he had been interstate on the exam day 'attending to family matters' with no mention of overseas business trips or medical problems. The university was now confronted with three totally different reasons for Herman's non-attendance at his accounting exam.

At a subsequent disciplinary hearing which Herman was invited to attend, he admitted that he had become confused about the events of the day in question and could not now precisely remember what he was doing. He did not look convincing.

Herman was suspended for one semester for his feeble attempts to avoid an examination and was warned that any future appearance before the committee would meet with sterner punishment.

CASES THAT MADE HEADLINES

Fax machines

Electronic pagers

Dishonest teachers

Murder

Cassette players

Mobile phones

Radio transmitters

Digital electronics

Watches

Calculators

Candidate substitution

Lowering standards

Suspicious results

Leaking exams

Plagiarism

Selling exam solutions

Stealing exam papers

Falsifying records

Forging marks

Fake degrees

Altering answers

Hand and foot signals

Cheating services

Demanding money

Burning vehicles

Underwear checks

Spy pen

Smuggling

Writing on body parts

Depressed lover

Using toilets

Bribing markers

Losing a PhD

Time-zone cheating

Breach of contract

Using weapons Intimidating supervisors

Sexual favours

Using loudhailers

Stone throwing

Flying faxes lead to prison

If God had intended us to fly, he would never have given us railways.
Michael Flanders, (attrib.)

In a disturbing case for those who rely on air travel, trainee pilots attending a Queensland flying school reportedly paid an instructor to fill out their written exams. A spokesman for the Guild of Air Pilots and Air Navigators said a flying-school instructor had been charged with cheating after investigations revealed that students had paid the instructor to complete exams faxed to the school by the Civil Aviation Authority. As a result of the deception, which occurred between 1991 and March 1992, the instructor was sentenced to three years in prison.

The spokesman added that in an apparent bungle, rather than through fraud, sample exams sent to student pilots to help them study turned out to be the real exam papers. A spokesman for the Australian Federation of Air Pilots, however, reportedly declared that fraud does arise in flying schools with pilots falsifying experience levels to gain licence qualifications for jobs. He claimed this was due to the intense competition for flying positions.

Friendly relations

If you steal from one author, it's plagiarism; if you steal from many, it's research.

Wilson Mizner

Examinations which took place during May 1994 in India's schools and colleges were subject to 'flying squads' of invigilators who moved from one exam hall to another to check that no student took crib sheets into the exam.

Despite their best efforts, there were many reports of crowds of friends and relations flocking outside exam halls, tossing books or slips of paper to students to help them answer questions. Tougher students placed knives on their desks to discourage invigilators from being too nosy.

To help minimise exam cheating, a state government, in a desperate move three years before, had passed an Act which provided harsh punishment, including imprisonment, for those caught cheating. As a result of massive student pro-tests, this Anti-Copying Act was repealed the following year.

Caught with their pants down

Colonel Cathcart had courage and never hesitated to volunteer his men for any target available.

Joseph Heller, Catch-22, *1961*

Acting on a tip-off, police in Bangkok arrested seventy-five students after they were found with radio receivers and batteries hidden in their underwear. Exactly how the devices were confiscated is left to the imagination, but those involved were charged with conspiring to cheat in a Thai army college entrance exam. The penalty for anyone found guilty of the offence was up to two years in prison.

The examination rooms were raided after the college sus-pected a plot to cheat, in the non-commissioned officers test. Without justifying the candidates' efforts, their actions were perhaps understandable given only 400 places were available and more than 10 000 people were sitting the exam. Such fierce competition meant that 96 per cent of examinees would be unsuccessful.

The suspects, who faced additional charges of operating illegal radio devices, confessed to police that they had paid up to 50 000 baht (US$2000) each to a policeman who sent them answers to questions from a transmitter. Subsequently, the policeman who sent the signals was also arrested, apparently having instructed each man to scratch his groin during the exam according to pre-arranged codes.

Principal unmasked

Headmasters have powers at their disposal with which Prime Ministers have never yet been invested.

Winston Churchill, My Early Life, *1930*

Three Japanese were caught cheating in the March 1991 entrance examination for an agricultural high school. In the normal course of events this would not have attracted much outside attention, except in this case one of the three caught red-handed with pencil and rubber was actually the headmaster of the school.

The headmaster and two senior teachers were arrested for allegedly doctoring the entrance exam papers of fifteen of 399 applicants for the school's 240 places. The headmaster later revealed to police that four 'influential people' had asked him to 'arrange' for their sons and others to pass the exams and he had been 'unable to decline' because of their influence in the agricultural industry.

It was alleged that in order to comply with the request, the three suspects spent several hours following the exam in the headmaster's office correcting wrong answers and filling in the blanks in the multiple choice papers to ensure that the fifteen students all passed. It was further reported that at the beginning of the tampering exercise they made some effort to disguise their own handwriting, but after a while they grew tired of this and simply reverted to their normal writing style.

Rape charge leads to violence

We are perplexed, but not in despair.

2 Corinthians 4:8

In a tragic case involving examinations, officials in southern Bangladesh said that at least forty people were injured in clashes between students and police after a policeman tried to rape a girl during college examinations. They reported that a member of a police squad who was engaged to stop cheating at an examination centre at Barisal became part of the problem when he sneaked into a ladies' toilet where he attempted to assault the student.

Fortunately the girl managed to fight her way out and returned to the exam room where she reported the incident to fellow examinees. Not surprisingly, this triggered a fierce battle between police and students. Despite the resulting violence, nobody was arrested although after the melee senior police officers did arrest one policeman on an attempted rape charge after the girl was able to identify him.

Failure leads to murder

I have found the best way to give advice to your children is to find out what they want and then advise them to do it.

Harry S. Truman, television interview, 1955

In what appeared at first to be a routine event, a 19-year-old college student in China was caught cheating in an English test and received a failing grade. The student, from an industrial engineering institute, had apparently let his academic work slip owing to a devotion to martial arts. This infatuation with his hobby greatly disturbed his parents, particularly since his father was a full professor and his mother an associate professor. In desperation, they drew up a 'contract' stating that they would not be prepared to pay his tuition for the following year unless he was able to obtain marks of 70 per cent in all his courses.

The father was also reported as saying that he would 'disown' his son if he failed the exams. The son signed the agreement, but under pressure the following semester he was caught cheating in an English exam. The college failed him and, despite a desperate attempt on his part to convince the examiners to allow him to sit another exam, he was refused permission.

To make matters worse, the school policy was to make cheating a matter of public record and note it on the candidate's academic files. The student, an only son, pleaded with his mother to be transferred to another college, but she refused to agree.

The story had a tragic ending as the student reportedly strangled his mother in the kitchen while she was washing. He then killed his sleeping father in the bedroom in the same way.

After these grisly incidents, he wandered in a number of cities, including Beijing and Shanghai, spent his savings of about 700 yuan (US$90), then returned home where he prepared to commit suicide. Before he could do so he was arrested and sentenced to death by the intermediate people's court of Nanjing.

Calculating cheats

Sattinger's Law: It works better if you plug it in.

Arthur Bloch, Murphy's Law and Other Reasons
Why Things Go Wrong, 1977

A Sydney university has foiled modern technology used to cheat the exam system by forbidding students to take their own calculators, mobile phones or Walkman-type portable cassette players into exams. The ruling did not come cheaply, however, since in 1993 the university purchased 3000 calculators for students to use in exams at an estimated cost of A$50 000 (US$37 000).

WHAT? THIS? IT'S A PENCIL

OHHH... YOU MEAN THAT!

An impressive range of electronics is available to the modern cheat and the administration was determined to keep one step ahead. First to be banished were mobile phones after one student alerted the university to attempts by a group of students to develop a way of linking the screen on a mobile phone to an outside telecommunications device. Messages could be received on mobile phones by students as they sat in the exam room.

Cassette players were also banished since there is no guarantee that the tapes inserted contain only music—there is the possibility that recorded information may also be included. There is also the chance that players could be two-way communication devices in disguise.

An academic revealed that supervisors had previously discovered hand-held computers with memories full of information being passed off as calculators. He noted that there are so many different kinds of calculators that this method of cheating was becoming impossible to detect.

Beep, beep!

I answer the phone 'Dickerson here' because I'm Dickerson and I'm here.

Charles Barsotti, Kings Don't Carry Money, *cartoon, 1981*

Not wanting to be out of action for even a moment, some students constantly keep in touch by means of electronic pagers. An additional use for such equipment was uncovered by two students in Beijing who were caught using the devices to cheat in their high school exams. In a noble gesture, one student completed his physics exam paper early and left the room, but instead of going home took up a position outside, near the window. From there he transmitted answers to his less academically inclined friend by means of a pager equipped to display Chinese characters.

Their teamwork may have gone undetected, except that the slower student drew attention to himself by repeatedly glancing into his shirt pocket before ever writing anything down. The pair subsequently admitted that this was not the first time that pagers had been used for cheating.

Parental pressure

The first half of our lives is ruined by our parents, and the second half by our children.

Clarence Darrow, inventor of the board game Monopoly

In some countries there is tremendous pressure on students and their families for children to gain entry to an appropriate college. Such is the case in South Korea where a university entrance examination fraud was uncovered resulting in more than fifty-eight people being arrested. Another university was suspected of having admitted more than sixty students by illegal means.

In one incident, police reported that a student from a much sought after university was offered US$13 000 to sit the entrance exam for another student. To make the deal even more attractive, the impostor was promised more money after the exam by his teacher who had secured over US$100 000 from the mother of the real exam candidate.

In another case, a senior state prosecutor resigned from his position after his son confessed he had sat entrance exams for several others. The tearful confession was made on national television.

Students come well prepared for exams

A rich man is nothing but a poor man with money.

W.C. Fields

Exam time in Bangladesh is regularly a nightmare for both students and officials alike when more than 600 000 students aged fifteen annually sit for school exams across the country. Police guard examination centres and ban non-students from entering. In April 1993 an official reported that 'students were found copying from prepared notes or textbooks. Some hid them under their vests or in their shirtsleeves or even in their shoes. Unscrupulous teachers supplied their students illegally.'

In addition, over fifty teachers were sacked for supplying notes to students. Another official declared:

> Examination fraud has become a national vice and fighting it has been an uphill task. Questions are leaked for money, teachers are bribed to help students illegally and even parents buy their children undue favours.

Moves by authorities to change the existing unsatisfactory exam procedures resulted in widespread protests by students, forcing the current system to be retained.

False accusations

All wrong-doing is done in the sincere belief that it is the best thing to do.

Arnold Bennett

In an unusual incident at a Sydney business college, a supervisor discovered several sheets of paper covered with written material strategically placed on a student's desk during an economics examination. When questioned, the student vigorously protested that the information was allowable formulae, but the supervisor remained unconvinced. To

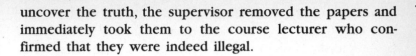

uncover the truth, the supervisor removed the papers and immediately took them to the course lecturer who confirmed that they were indeed illegal.

The supervisor then returned to the exam room where she confronted the alleged culprit at his desk. However, the student challenged denied it was him she had previously spoken to and claimed she had mistaken him for the student who had been sitting two seats behind but had since left the exam room.

The supervisor was convinced that she had correctly identified the culprit and reported him to the dean. After intensive questioning of the student and a review of statements made by student witnesses, it became apparent that the supervisor had indeed made an error in her identification. However, this was not before the accused, in his frustration, had smashed his glasses against a brick wall.

Needless to say there were humble apologies from many quarters. The real villain was never identified since no specific seat numbers were allocated to students.

Teacher murdered by students

If the desire to kill and the opportunity to kill came always together, who would escape hanging?

Mark Twain

In a replay of similar incidents of previous years, a teacher in Bangladesh was hacked to death in July 1995 trying to stop cheating in the nationwide secondary school exams. Police reported savage fighting in the Narail district where hundreds of students were injured in running battles with monitors.

Teachers and police were outnumbered by students, parents and supporters who attacked them, resulting in hundreds of people sustaining injuries, some serious. In the first week alone, 4000 students were expelled for cheating or attacking monitors, while some teachers were suspended for trying to illegally help students.

In one incident at Dhaka Medical College, the exams had to be postponed because students unhappy at having to sit for them set off home-made bombs. It was also reported that twenty students were able to get themselves admitted to Dhaka University without passing the required entrance exams.

Remarkable results

Who shall decide when doctors disagree?

Alexander Pope

An outstanding case of coincidence occurred at a small provincial medical school in the Philippines when students there startled the academic world by capturing twenty-two of the top twenty-six places in the nationwide exams. The government ordered an investigation into the results since the students had beaten candidates from the country's best schools. Suspicions were heightened when it was learned that seventy-nine of the eighty-two college graduates managed to pass the exam, including many who scored over 95 per cent in subjects considered to be extremely difficult.

Students vigorously denied that questions were leaked to them in advance and some subsequently appeared in public with placards that read 'No miracles, just brains'. Moreover, they have rejected suggestions that they take new tests to prove the high marks they scored were genuine, since they claimed that this would simply be an admission of guilt.

Tune in for the latest

Well, if I called the wrong number, why did you answer the phone?

James Thurber, cartoon in the New Yorker

It may not be considered particularly unusual to talk to oneself from time to time, but students in Hong Kong were warned to keep their mouths closed during a particular English exam. In this case, students were examined by answering questions which were broadcast over the radio, with students required to supply their own radios. Unfortunately, it turned out that radios weren't the only things the students took into the exam room.

An alert to supervisors followed the impressive antics of one student who managed to remove the cassette mechanism from a personal radio–cassette player and replace it with a mobile phone. He listened to the questions from the radio, then made telephone calls to a friend who relayed the answers. This led to the checking of all equipment for hidden tapes and a complete ban on muttering during the paper.

Interestingly, a similar exam had previously resulted in a directive to supervisors not to pace up and down during the question time. In one case, the students found that the supervisors were acting as aerials and the reception would change each time a supervisor walked past, with the result that students found themselves tuning into a variety of radio stations.

Overall, 1900 out of 300 000 students were penalised for 'irregular practices' during the exam. A regretful spokesman said 'of these, 572 had brought in an illegal calculator while 399 candidates went to the wrong exam centre. Usually they offered the excuse that they had slept in.'

Nursing exams for sale

After two days in hospital, I took a turn for the nurse.

W.C. Fields

When exam officials feel that some form of mass cheating may have taken place in an important exam, the only real solution is to require everyone to retake the paper. Following the 1995 Thai national entrance examination for nurses, the Thailand Public Health Ministry ordered the results cancelled throughout the country after discovering that the exam papers had been leaked. This calamity involved 50 000 students who had to sit for the exams again in 79 exam centres.

Even with this drastic measure, the Deputy Permanent Secretary was apprehensive that the offenders would leak the papers again because of the money that could be earned and the lenient punishments often ordered by the courts. Police suspected that the papers were sold for large sums of money to be transferred into numbered bank accounts once students passed the exam. Those involved apparently have agents throughout Thailand.

In what sounded like an admission of defeat, the Permanent Secretary was quoted as saying that it was impossible to ensure that there is no cheating at all.

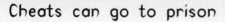

Cheats can go to prison

I'll never forget my mother's words to me when I first went to jail. She said, 'Hello son'.

Eric Morecombe and Ernie Wise, The Morecombe and Wise Joke Book, *1979*

After years of examination irregularities and cheating, a 1991 cabinet meeting in Bangladesh decided to introduce harsh penalties of up to ten years imprisonment for students guilty of offences such as copying from textbooks and changing answer scripts. Similar penalties were also to apply to teachers who leaked exam questions, issued false marks or diploma certificates or supplied notes for examinees.

Witnesses and officials in schools reported that students expelled for cheating often attacked teachers, tore up examination papers, burned furniture, set vehicles on fire and clashed with police. In fact, during one exam period, junior students from several schools had stoned cars, beat passers-by and let off firecrackers in the street in anticipation of the proposed changes to the examination system.

Indeed, final exams held by one education board were cancelled three times after questions were leaked and sold openly. Police suspected teachers of the leaking as well as supplying answers inside examination halls for money.

Prophetically, one police officer said: 'The government is now trying a last resort. Let us see how it works.' Sadly its efforts were in vain since, as a result of student protests, the old system was reinstated within two years.

Crackdown plummets pass rates

For every person wishing to teach, there are thirty not wanting to be taught.

Anon.

Sometimes the extent of the cheating that takes place in examinations can only be guessed at, but a story from Cambodia highlights the difficulties faced by authorities there. With the introduction two years previously of an anti-corruption campaign by concerned officials, the pass rate in the 1994 high school exams plummeted from the usual 70 to 80 per cent to just over 4 per cent.

It had been suspected that irregularities mainly stemmed from the actions of underpaid teachers who were reportedly giving pass marks in return for bribes from students. The result of the crackdown was that only 751 out of 17 783 students in grade 11 managed to pass their baccalaureate exams. The Education Minister was quoted as saying he believed the exams now reflected 'no corruption at all'.

Watch out for the answer

I've been on a calendar, but never on time.

Marilyn Monroe, Look, *1962*

During a college entrance examination, a Thai student came under close scrutiny resulting in his over-optimistic scheme being uncovered. The culprit repeatedly glanced at his watch, an action that naturally attracted the attention of a vigilant supervisor who demanded a closer inspection. The student protested that his preoccupation with his watch was merely because he was very concerned about the amount of time he had left to finish his questions.

However, it was discovered that the watch was actually a radio-pager that had been modified to contain illegal information. The student, aged 20, was arrested and detained by police.

Killers for hire

What's a thousand dollars? Mere chicken feed. A poultry matter.
                                                    Groucho Marx

It was reported in 1991 that hundreds of Chinese students, desperate to leave the country, were cheating at English language tests to gain a university place overseas. One former Beijing University student, now a government translator, said that many Chinese students pay a skilled English speaker to take the test in their place. This practice is known as 'hiring a killer'.

The phoney candidates are paid according to how well they perform in the examinations. For example, gaining a grade high enough to win university admission would net around

1000 yuan (US$125) while a scholarship-winning score would earn around 2000 yuan (US$250). The average annual urban income is about 1300 yuan (US$160).

Keep your shirt on

Women's clothes: never wear anything that panics the cat.
P. J. O'Rourke, Modern Manners, *1983*

Some students become so angry when they are accused of cheating that they instinctively lash out at the accuser. This can be the case whether the person is guilty or innocent. Indeed, one female student in an examination centre southwest of Dhaka became furious when an exam supervisor expelled her from the classroom when she was caught copying from textbooks.

To make matters worse, apart from being in the unfortunate position of being accused of cheating, her temper got the better of her and she decided to throw the first thing she could lay her hands on at the supervisor. Since she was apparently reluctant to remove any of her clothing, she hurled her shoes in the supervisor's direction.

As a result police were called and the nineteen-year-old was arrested and taken to jail where it was left to her parents to apply for bail.

Gun pulled on lecturer

Teachers are overworked and underpaid. True, it is an exacting and exhausting business, this damming up the flood of human potentialities.
George B. Leonard, Education and Fantasy

Supervisors have to be careful when accusing a student of cheating during an examination. If an examinee is hauled out of a test and is later found to be innocent, the stigma attached to the event by witnessing students can be very hard to overcome. That is, exonerated or not, there will always be those who have some doubts about the integrity of the victim.

An extreme case occurred when a Cambodian student sitting for an economics examination was accused of cheating by his lecturer. Instead of expressing his disquiet by shouting or arguing, the candidate responded by pulling out a pistol and threatening to kill his accuser, a staff member from the French Embassy. The French Embassy submitted a formal protest to the Foreign Affairs and Education ministries over the incident which occurred in the faculty of Economic Sciences.

Understandably, the Embassy would not allow French staff to work again in the college until security had been tightened.

Broadcast news

Some microphones work great as long as you blow into them. So you stand there like an idiot blowing and saying, 'Are we on? Can you hear me?' Everyone admits they can hear you blowing. It's only when you speak that the microphone goes dead.

Erma Bombeck, If Life is a Bowl of Cherries,
What Am I Doing in the Pits?, *1978*

There are some cases of cheating when not only the candidates are involved. Sometimes, a helpful teacher may participate and in other instances the corruption extends to the exam supervisors. In one example of mass co-operation, it was found that no fewer than twenty-one Chinese teachers and officials had assisted a middle school student to cheat in the annual national college entrance examination.

Using a miniature microphone hidden in his clothes, the student had reportedly transmitted details of the test questions from the examination room to his brothers, both officials in Hebei Province. They recorded the questions and arranged for teachers to supply them with the correct answers. These were then placed in the men's room in the school, to be collected by corrupt exam supervisors. Once they had retrieved the answers, the supervisors took them to the examination room where they were quietly given to the student.

The scheme was uncovered by three teachers not involved in the plot who picked up the microphone signals while innocently listening to the radio. This scheme was reportedly the first detected case of cheating involving the use of a microphone in the national college entrance examination in China.

Exams locked away for safe-keeping

A general and a bit of shooting makes you forget your troubles . . . it takes your mind off the cost of living.

Brendan Behan, The Hostage, *1958*

The chairman of a government-sponsored school in India was reported in 1991 as declaring that 'greasing the palms of the examiners' was standard practice at the public exams. He added that 'there was a time when question papers were leaked to students for a flat fee of 2000 rupees (US$100) per copy and only stopped when we started keeping the papers in the bank vaults'.

'Teachers make money from internal school exams by encouraging private tuition as a kind of ransom which is often directly linked to the success of their pupils,' the chairman reportedly said. 'An average teacher earning 2000 rupees (US$100) per month could multiply their income six-fold by tutoring four students at 100 rupees (US$5) per hour.'

Although he, and other educators, favoured the idea of a continual assessment system to avoid emphasis on exams, universities apparently did not accept this method.

Persistence pays off

Thieves respect property; they merely wish the property to become their property that they may perfectly respect it.

G.K. Chesterton, The Man Who Was Thursday, *1908*

If a student has successfully managed to cheat the system on one occasion, then there is every chance that a further attempt will be made. In a long-running scheme operating in China, a group of students from a textile training school were found to have stolen examination papers for three consecutive years before finally being tracked down by school authorities.

It was reported that a total of eighteen students and two workers were involved in the final theft of test papers, while thirty-five other students had also managed to see the papers before the exams. An investigation revealed that from the first semester three years previously, the students had been breaking into a locked room where the exam papers were kept.

With such an appalling lack of security, the culprits managed to copy papers, steal them outright or simply remove the stencil that contained the test questions. Flushed with success, two years later they had expanded their operation by collaborating with the person operating the duplicator along with a typist.

Inspector gadget revisited

Technology has brought meaning to the lives of many technicians.

Ed Bluestone, The National Lampoon Encyclopaedia of Humor, *1973*

Some exam officials long for the good old days when all they had to worry about was the occasional crib sheet smuggled up someone's sleeve or down their socks. Unfortunately things aren't that easy these days, as highlighted by the report from an analyst in the Post and Telegraph Department in Thailand. He lamented that in days gone by it used to be a relatively simple matter to purchase a set of correct answers for the fiercely competitive university entrance examinations. However, this had all changed with students resorting to the 'sort of high-technology gadgetry most people only see in James Bond movies'.

He added that 'cheating is getting really sophisticated. Students are now doing it by radio.' To make matters worse, they were not simply content with old-fashioned miniature radios and earphones—they had decided to use the latest in digital electronics.

'We think they use receivers that don't make a sound—possibly even pressure devices on the skin,' said the analyst. The Thai Universities Ministry was so concerned that the 80 000 candidates should have an equal chance in the entrance examinations that sophisticated detection and jamming devices were dispatched to campuses administering the tests.

The analyst normally worked in an extremely sensitive area—so much so that he requested that reporters only use a pseudonym for him.

Help is only a stone's throw away

The quickest way to end a war is to lose it.

George Orwell, Shooting an Elephant, *1950*

Given little choice, the state-run Central Board for Secondary Education (CBSE) cancelled examinations at seven centres in New Delhi in July 1991 after newspapers gave eyewitness accounts of mass cheating while invigilators looked on.

Question papers were reportedly smuggled outside the exam rooms to waiting parents who passed them on to experts who had been hired for the occasion. Answer sheets were then wrapped around stones and tossed back through open windows. Meanwhile, other examinations proceeded with police attempting to enforce a ban on crowds congregating around the schools.

The chairman of the CBSE was quoted as saying there were 'some instances of parents and friends of the examinees who shouted out answers from loudhailers near the schools. This is only the tip of the iceberg.' The police found it necessary to issue a circular banning 'carrying of arms, cudgels, swords, guns, knives, sticks or any other articles that are capable of being used for causing physical violence'.

In some Indian states it was reported that students often enter exam centres brandishing knives at invigilators.

I was just obeying orders

You can't help liking the boss. If you don't, they fire you.

Anon.

If you want to get on in the world it is wise to keep on the good side of those in the organisation who are above you. However, if a superior asked you to do something illegal, most people would draw the line. In one instance, an intimidated worker in China caved in under intense pressure from above and became involved in a scheme that eventually came unstuck.

During January 1986 it was reported that party cadres (supporters) were doing everything they could to obtain college diplomas, even resorting to cheating and purchasing false qualifications. In an interesting example of harmonious relationships in the workplace, an automobile engine factory superintendent in Shenyang (formerly Mukden) forced his better-educated subordinate to take his place in a two-and-a-half-year correspondence course in business administration, which would ultimately lead to a college degree. When the time came for the superintendent to sit for the final examinations, he made his assistant take them instead.

It was probably divine justice that the substitute candidate unfortunately failed one of the tests. Undeterred, the superintendent rectified the situation by having the examination-paper grader add ten marks to his score so as to make up a passing grade, resulting in the awarding of his coveted diploma. However, the cheating scam was eventually discovered and the factory superintendent was fired.

In another incident, a party deputy secretary in Shaanxi (formerly Shensi) Province also acquired a university diploma with the assistance of a subordinate. The party cadre then asked the university to reissue a diploma, claiming that his original diploma was 'lost during the cultural revolution'. His forgery was discovered and he was dismissed.

Attacking the problem

I'll never forget my first fight . . . all of a sudden I found someone I knew in the fourth row. It was me.

Henny Youngman, 1940

It is a source of irritation to some students that exam cheating is illegal and some will go to great lengths to maintain what they believe is their 'right'. In a violent incident in Bangladesh, a student punched a magistrate for not allowing him to copy from his text at an examination centre near Chittagong port. An official reported that the student, assisted by his friends, managed to lock the magistrate and some teachers into an adjacent building and beat them up until police were able to rescue them.

Police said that students attacked them with guns, knives, sticks and stones and they retaliated by firing into the crowd. As a result, nearly seventy people were injured including thirteen who sustained bullet wounds. The previous week, students had gone on the rampage at several test centres outside Dhaka after they were caught with prepared notes supplied by friends or relatives.

Around 6000 of the 340 000 students sitting for exams were expelled for cheating and violence. In addition, at least two teachers were sacked for helping students copy from textbooks or notes.

Long hair hides headphones

Why don't you get a haircut? You look like a chrysanthemum.

P.G. Wodehouse

In the days before electronic pagers and mobile phones were readily available, some students relied on citizen band (CB) radios to obtain information during exams. This assistance did not always come cheaply, as evidenced by a police report from Taiwan stating that five students each paid TW$35 000 (US$1250) to subscribe to a cheating service.

The students managed to smuggle their own CB radios or scanners into the exam room and tuned into the channel of a tipster who fed them answers via his own CB radio as they took a national college entrance examination. The accomplice was a college student who rented a hotel room a short distance from the exam site and broadcast the exam hints and answers to the five high school students.

A police official remarked that 'all the high school students had long hair to conceal the earphones they were wearing'. The ring was exposed after the police department's electronics surveillance unit in Eastern Taiwan picked up powerful signals emitting from the hotel. Detectives arrested the culprit running the radio transmitter and then arrested the five students as they came to the hotel suite.

The students were charged with breaking the communications control law, which outlaws the use of CB radios without a permit.

Rejection causes depression

A promiscuous person is one who is getting more sex than you.

Victor Lownes, Playboy, *1985*

The love-lorn have a special place in the annals of cheating, as typified by the student at a British university who felt that his exam performance wasn't up to his usual standard. Indeed, he had failed rather miserably. He explained to his mathematics professor that he had been lusting after a certain female who he knew had been 'sleeping around' and therefore had assumed that she would sleep with anybody.

However, apparently her preferences did not extend to himself, since despite numerous overtures he was unable to persuade the young lady to co-operate. This rejection had significantly lowered his morale and severely hampered his concentration. He requested that he be allowed to sit for a supplementary exam when he had had time to 'pull himself together'. Although there was no doubt that his confidence had been shattered by the woman in question, his case was not considered by examiners to warrant special treatment.

Shake a leg

He told her that her stockings were wrinkled. The trouble was, she wasn't wearing any.

Anon.

A first year civil engineering student at a British university described a bizarre incident of exam cheating. He explained that 'there was this girl sitting next to me wearing stockings and suspenders. She unclasped the suspenders, rolled her stocking down to her knee and she had a whole essay written on her thigh. She copied the whole thing out.'

However, such antics are not restricted to women. Another university reported the case of a male student who turned up for an exam in cold weather, wearing baggy shorts. Examiners soon discovered an array of formulae written all over his thighs. The university officials were so alarmed by this occurrence that they were moved to issue special leaflets and start a poster campaign warning of the penalties for cheating.

Colourful Cambridge

It's only a step down from the sublime to the ridiculous.
Napoleon Bonaparte

In an inspiring signal to other institutions, Cambridge University, one of the pinnacles of British learning, adopted a policy in May 1995 of using coloured paper for examination answers. This innovation was designed to outwit candidates planning to smuggle in prepared essays or crib sheets.

To make life difficult, cheats now have to guess the colour of the stationery—randomly selected from lilac, lime green, pink or sky blue rather than the standard white-lined material—supplied during the exam. If they want to rely on answers written in advance, they have to take a punt on the colour to be used, or else have written on paper of each of the possible colours. They would then face the risky proposition of sorting the papers during the exam.

This pioneering move was prompted by a classics student caught cheating after a supervisor grew suspicious because his papers were folded unusually. The student was watched carefully during his next exam and was seen to slip from his jacket essays written in advance on official examination stationery.

Apparently the candidate added a few paragraphs that referred directly to the question during the exam as a 'final polish to the pre-written essays'. His punishment was suspension for a year. Although examinations in classics were allegedly renowned for their predictability, the offender was the only one caught cheating from a total of over 10 000 students who sat for exams.

An examinations officer was quoted as saying that the new measure would 'put the wind up anyone who might just consider bringing in prepared answers as a way out of a possible scrape'.

Roll-on answers

Mark my words, when a society has to resort to the lavatory for humour, the writing is on the wall.

Alan Bennett, Forty Years On, *1968*

One British student admitted that he had cheated in an exam by meticulously copying various snippets of French vocabulary onto the inside of a cardboard lavatory roll which he put in place of the original one in the toilet cubicle assigned for examinees' use. Despite a thorough check of the cubicle by the supervisors, this clever piece of subterfuge went undetected and the offender was able to comfortably retrieve the information when necessary. In fact, the toilet paper manufacturer had possibly made his task easier since, in recent years, the size of the cardboard insert reportedly has been growing, perhaps to help hide the fact that there are fewer sheets of paper on the roll!

Another student, answering a genuine call of nature during an exam, was surprised to discover slabs of text carefully written in permanent marker pen on the inside of the toilet bowl itself. Next to the chain was a pleading note that read

'Please don't flush!'. It wouldn't have really mattered if he had, since the pen used was not water soluble.

Legal matters

I don't think you can make a lawyer honest by an act of legislature. You've got to work on his conscience. And his lack of conscience is what makes him a lawyer.

Will Rogers, 1927

Law students have a special place in the annals of exam dishonesty since it would seem that they, above all others, should have the utmost regard for the rules. However, a female law student in Britain was discovered referring to a pile of revision notes halfway through her final exams. After pleas of extenuating circumstances, a disciplinary committee allowed her to graduate with a pass degree.

In an interesting reversal of roles, the other students were reportedly furious at this decision. They argued that their work and achievement was being cheapened as a result. The student in question apparently continued her studies with the aim of becoming a barrister.

Dentists are on time

I've got a tooth that's driving me to extraction.

Charlie McCarthy (Edgar Bergen), NBC Radio, 1937

Many universities go to considerable lengths to ensure that students do not smuggle illegal material into the exam room, with special attention often given to the types of calculator students plan to use. However, an everyday part of students' normal attire can easily be overlooked by supervisors.

This was the case in France when health professionals were caught up in a scandal involving their wristwatches. The scheme involved fourth year dentistry students who concluded that there would not be a close inspection of their watches and that they would be the ideal means to smuggle notes into the exam. The students managed to conceal strips of microfiche containing vital information between their watches and their wrists.

Their efforts were in vain, however, since they were detected and the entire group of seventy students had their marks cancelled. As a result, the group had to sit for another exam, this time without any assistance.

A little help from friends

He's a distinguished man of letters. He works for the Post Office.
Max Kauffmann

Some lecturers are asking for trouble when they set their classes 'take-home' exams that are worth a substantial part of the assessment. This type of exam usually involves the candidates taking the examination paper away from the exam room, completing the questions elsewhere and returning their answers at a later date.

For some students, the temptation to gain assistance from others is too great to resist, despite their having to provide assurances that any work submitted is entirely their own. In October 1994, a member of the Council of Senate of a prestigious British university reported that take-home exam papers to assess master's degree courses in international relations had led to a 'disturbing outbreak of cheating'.

A graduate who tutored in the course said that the problem came under notice when one of his students asked him to review her examination script, and he discovered that the term 'review' can have a multitude of meanings. The tutor stated that the student initially claimed only to want help with her English and phrasing, but soon made it quite clear that she also wanted him to rewrite the paper for money. When he refused, she told the tutor that others in the department had friends assisting in some capacity or another. An interesting comment from one student was that international relations people 'bum around—they party all the time'.

Critics of take-home exams claim that the assessment system, where students have three days to complete the final exam, 'almost invites collaboration and irregularity'.

English student makes history

I was a modest good-humoured boy. It is Oxford that has made me insufferable.

Max Beerbohm, 'Going Back to School'

Of growing concern to academics is the extent of plagiarism that occurs in essays submitted for assessment. The problem usually involves substantial quantities of material that has either been directly copied or paraphrased from a source that has not been cited.

In only the third case of plagiarism uncovered at Oxford University this century, a student was stripped of his doctorate in philosophy in 1994 for copying sections of a previously published text. The student, who was enrolled from 1982 to 1986, lost his title after his former supervisor was alerted to similarities between the thesis he submitted on eighteenth-century American politics and material that had been published by Princeton University in the United States.

His supervisor was quoted as saying that at the time he had been surprised by the great improvement in his student's work but 'I suppose I attributed this to my teaching'. A similar case occurred at Oxford University in 1990 when a student was found guilty of plagiarising sections of his doctoral thesis from work already published by others in an academic journal.

Timed out

Meetings . . . are rather like cocktail parties. You don't want to go, but you're cross not to be asked.

Jilly Cooper, How to survive from Nine to Five, *1970*

Examinations can take many forms and the term may be broadened to include any competition involving a test of skills. On some occasions it is not the participants who are accused of illegal practices, but the officials.

In an unusual allegation of cheating, a former British national champion scrabble player claimed that he was cheated out of four minutes of valuable playing time when his timing clock was started while he was visiting the toilet. He went on to lose the tournament.

Apparently the player headed for the lavatory during a closely fought eleven-game contest. He reportedly had to fight his way through five crowded reception rooms where a number of meetings were in progress. 'The only toilets were on the ground floor', he said and 'a convention of cowboys and cowgirls had booked the hotel for the week-end and were using most of the rooms. Many of these people were inside since it was raining heavily and I had to wait until one of the cubicles was free.'

During the unfortunate toilet break, which according to the player had lasted seven minutes, the player's opponent raced to an early advantage by scoring 76 points with the word 'scanners'. The aggrieved player decided to sue tournament officials, who had started the clock after three minutes, for damages and lost prize money. In court he claimed that the officials did not allow sufficient time for the 'call of nature'.

I spy

Variety is the life of spies.

Anon.

Those with money to spare now have the welcome opportunity to arm themselves with the latest wizardry in spy technology. There is a dazzling range of equipment available, including cameras that can be disguised as credit cards and pens that act as miniature tape recorders. These pens can be left casually in the office of a rival or colleague and record any conversation that takes place. Later, when the pen is retrieved the owner is much better informed as to exactly what people are planning or thinking.

A number of shops in London specialise in covert equipment. In 1995, an enterprising English student impressed with hi-tech gadgetry purchased a pen incorporating a tiny transmitter (including a cordless earpiece) from one such store and used it to relay questions outside the examination hall to an accomplice who fed back the answers.

The store spokesman said that although the device had cost the student about £2000 (US$3000), he had been particularly pleased with his purchase and had taken the trouble to ring the store from overseas to report how well he had performed in his exams using his new pen.

Harsh penalties in Italy

She said that all the sights in Rome were named after London cinemas.

Nancy Mitford, Pigeon Pie, *1940*

A student who is found guilty of cheating at university can expect to face punishment ranging from a warning to failure in a subject to permanent exclusion from the institution. It is rare for the university to call in outside authorities since it is usually thought preferable to deal with such matters internally.

However, severe punishment was handed out in Italy when a court sentenced sixty-five staff and graduates of Rome's la Sapienza University to up to seven years in jail for illegally purchasing degrees. The court heard that the economics and science students had paid an average of 450 000 lire (US$275) each to 'pass' exams for which they never sat. The discovery of the scheme prompted a wider enquiry into suspected result-rigging among 1000 graduates of other la Sapienza faculties.

The most severe jail sentences, ranging from thirty months to seven years, were imposed on two university administrative staff members, two porters and a former student. The sixty 'graduates' were given jail terms of twelve to thirty-five months as well as being stripped of their degrees.

UNITED STATES OF AMERICA

Sex used to entice

Prostitution gives a girl an opportunity to meet people. It provides fresh air and wholesome exercise, and it keeps her out of trouble.
Joseph Heller, Catch-22, *1961*

A radio station in the United States reported that 'boosters' paid sorority women to have sex with football recruits to a university and hired other students to take tests for athletes. The broadcaster quoted unidentified sources as saying two sorority members were initially paid $400 a weekend to have sex with football prospects. He added that, over a period of years, the number of women grew to 'another six, eight and then ten girls involved'.

The women allegedly lured the athletes with the promise of more sex if they signed with the university, and endeavoured to obtain information about what other schools were offering them. It was stated that the organiser of the sex-for-athletes scheme had 'long since left school' and worked for a law firm. However, although the sexual favours plan which had started five years earlier had lapsed for a couple of years when the organiser departed, it had resumed on a larger scale and more women became involved.

It was also alleged that in addition to money, the women received extra gifts including a Mercedes-Benz car, the use of a fur coat for one year and a credit card. Other females were also reportedly recruited by boosters for different purposes including taking tests, stealing exams and writing papers for athletes. In addition, it was said that secretaries in various professors' offices were paid to alter the grades of football players before they were sent to the registrar's office, although most professors were not aware of the grade-fixing changes.

Reports of the scheme surfaced when university officials acknowledged they were investigating rumours from an anonymous tipster.

Quacks cause a scandal

Doctors think a lot of patients are cured who have simply quit in disgust.

Don Herold, playwright

Since it involves a profession that affects almost everybody, it was disturbing to read a report which followed a six-month Congressional investigation into false medical credentials. It was revealed that more than 10 000 people in the United States were suspected by law enforcement agencies and professional groups of possessing bogus medical degrees. A report on the investigation also said that federal student loan programs had been used to underwrite part of the fraud and about twenty million dollars in federal and state funds were being funnelled to diploma brokers and foreign medical schools participating in falsifying credentials.

The Chairman of the House Health Subcommittee declared that its data indicated 'the largest medical scandal in recent memory. We found evidence that some people posing as doctors have not even graduated from high school.' He added that investigators had also uncovered several groups of diploma brokers operating in the United States. He also said there was

> evidence that tests used to screen foreign medical graduates had been stolen, sold and made available for purchase before the exam, as well as extensive evidence of on-site cheating, substitution of exam takers

and other forms of deception. It is likely we will never know how many 'chequebook' doctors are in practice, but we estimate that more than 10 000 physicians with questionable credentials are practising in the United States.

In a related matter, the FBI announced the arrest and indictment of the operator of a company that placed newspaper advertisements of the type:

> College diplomas—one day. Has your diploma been lost or damaged? Most schools available. Beautiful exacting reproductions, including seals and colours. All inquiries confidential.

Schools counterfeited reportedly included Harvard, Pennsylvania State University and the North Carolina, Michigan and Colorado universities.

Police candidates cause uproar

I have never seen a situation so dismal that a policeman couldn't make it worse.

Brendan Behan (attrib.)

If there was one group in the community that you might expect would cause little trouble during examinations it is the police. However, this was far from the case when a fight broke out during a police qualification exam in Madison Square Garden, people talked over cellular phones and at least one man filled out another person's test.

With admirable concern for his students, a County College faculty member had decided to sit for the exam partly to see what his students had to face. Among the incidents that he witnessed were candidates—impatient at a delay of more than an hour before the test started—doing 'the wave', test supervisors who not only ignored people talking but even chatted among themselves and a supervisor falling asleep.

HA! IT'S PROGRAMMABLE ALL RIGHT!

More than 25 000 applicants sat for the exam that had been delayed by legal proceedings arising from charges that the test was biased against women and minorities.

Double play in the USA

A verbal agreement isn't worth the paper it's written on.

Louis B. Mayer (attrib.)

From time to time students involve themselves in schemes that they hope will improve their chances of passing exams, although on occasions they can come unstuck. In a most unusual incident, a female student in Pennsylvania claimed to have hired another student to sit for an examination in her place. In return, she had given the impostor a stereo valued at $1200.

The scam itself was undetected and all might have gone well except that the substitute candidate managed to fail the exam. The outraged student filed a complaint with the

118   EXAM SCAMS

police claiming that since a contract had not been fulfilled they should try and recover her property on her behalf.

Not surprisingly, university authorities reported that they had no idea who the women involved were.

Trouble at sea

The navy is a very gentlemanly business. You fire at the horizon to sink a ship and then you pull people out of the water and say 'Frightfully sorry, old chap'.

William Golding, The Sunday Times, *1984*

A major cheating scandal involving seventy-one midshipmen in the graduating class, took place at the United States Naval Academy, resulting in a special review board convened by the Pentagon recommending the expulsion of twenty-nine students and lesser punishment for the other forty-two.

The trouble began with the theft and copying of a difficult electrical engineering paper with some cadets claiming to have seen copies circulating in the academy's dormitory before the exam date. They subsequently alerted authorities who began an inquiry that resulted in months of hearings that significantly lowered morale on the campus in Annapolis, Maryland. The academy's honour code stated that midshipmen must not lie, cheat or steal.

After sixteen months of investigation, a navy report issued two years later found that the exam had been widely distributed in advance to up to 134 out of 700 midshipmen. It added that more than half of the accused confessed, while the rest 'repeatedly lied until confronted with the irrefutable proof of their involvement'.

Teacher leaks questions

He who can does. He who cannot, teaches.
George Bernard Shaw, Maxims for Revolutionists, *1903*

A helpful private high school teacher was dismissed for giving his students questions from the national advanced placement test when, a week before the history component, he handed out a 'review' sheet to seven students.

The principal of the school reported that:

> there was almost a 100 per cent correlation on the review sheet to the questions that were asked on the exam. There were four essay questions and 70 multiple choice questions on the review sheet. The order they were presented in was different, but the questions were almost identical.

Interestingly, it was left to an observant student to uncover the plot when he noticed that the cellophane wrap on his test had been torn. In a related incident, the night before the test one of the seven students faxed a copy of the review sheet to a friend at another high school, resulting in two students there also seeing the questions before taking the test.

The outcome was that all nine students had to take the test again.

Time zone cheating

Men talk of killing time, while time quietly kills them.
Dion Boucicault, Irish playwright and actor

On those occasions when students sit for national examinations in a number of states, the time zone differences across the country can result in some students finishing their papers before others actually commence. Normally this would not be a problem, but honour students at a United

States high school were investigated for reportedly being involved in a 'time zone cheating' scandal.

It was alleged that a student capitalised on the time zone difference to call a friend at another high school and feed him the essay questions from the advanced placement test on American history. A spokesman for the testing service said that he could recall only one other instance of 'time zone cheating' in his eleven years with the testing company.

In a separate incident in another state, a student was allowed to sit for her final exam in economics on a Friday, instead of the following Monday when all other students were taking the exam. She convinced authorities that immediately following the exam she would be heading for the airport to fly overseas in order to attend the funeral of a close friend on the Saturday.

Her circumstances seemed plausible enough, and indeed that is exactly what she did. However, on the Sunday she took the welcome opportunity to fax back to her friends a list of questions that would be in their exam the next day. It was only when a conscience-stricken student reported the arrangement to the lecturer the next morning that the test paper was postponed and a fresh one organised.

Hit-man hired

Murder is always a mistake . . . one should never do anything that one cannot talk about after dinner.

Oscar Wilde, The Picture of Dorian Gray, *1891*

There are times when even normally good students become desperate in their desire to achieve high marks in their exams. Not only might this involve some form of cheating, but in some cases extreme measures may be adopted.

In one such case, an honours student at a university college of law was arrested and charged with attempting to hire a hit-man to kill a law school secretary, along with her husband of twenty-three years. It was alleged that the second year student was accused by the secretary of obtaining a copy of an exam before it was administered.

According to court documents the student said: 'If I don't take this person out of the picture, I'm just screwed'. It was also reported that she was an excellent student who was in the top 10 per cent of her class. The reason for wanting her husband dead was unknown at the time.

Recycled questions

I have a memory like an elephant. In fact, elephants often consult me.
Noel Coward (attrib.)

There are times when lecturers marking examination papers are taken aback by an outstanding performance from a student who has not previously displayed any talent for the subject. It is not uncommon in such cases to check the handwriting on the test paper against other work known to be written by the student to determine if a substitute candidate has been used.

The Graduate Record Exam (GRE), administered by the Educational Testing Service (ETS), can be of great importance to any student who wishes to undertake graduate studies. It is possible to legitimately purchase books with sample questions or even to seek the assistance of a coaching company to try to obtain a higher mark. However, the staff of one such company became curious when they started hearing the same questions on the new computerised version over and over again from students who had requested assistance.

The company suspected that perhaps the examiners were recycling some of their questions, in which case enterprising students could memorise the questions and possibly sell them or distribute them on the Internet. To test their hypothesis, the company sent three employees undercover to take the test and memorise as many questions as they could. In doing so they created a replica test and sent it to the ETS.

So successful were their efforts that they managed to match up between 70 to 80 per cent of the actual GRE questions. As a result the GRE tests were suspended pending further investigation.

Note takers clean up

I love being a writer. What I can't stand is the paperwork.
Peter De Vries

Sometimes the effort of attending lectures (particularly boring ones) is just too much for some of today's modern students. Such an attitude was used to advantage by two enterprising former state university students who commenced a 'note taking' service. Under the scheme, students could avoid lectures and simply pay up to $30 for class lecture notes. So successful was the operation that within three years it had extended to eighty-three different classes.

Note takers for the service are screened beforehand and must have a Grade Point Average (GPA) of at least 3.2 and be registered in the course. The notes, mainly for lower-level courses with at least 100 students, are neatly typed and copied onto red paper to cut back on subsequent copying. A spokesman for the service is reported as saying: 'I'm sure a large majority [of subscribers] are slack students. I've sold a whole semester pack, 70 pages, to a person a half hour before the exam. That's just being slack.'

The service does not encourage cheating but may well save students inventing excuses for not having lecture notes. It is disappointing that so many of them appear to gain very little out of actual attendance at their classes.

Cheating widespread

Football isn't a matter of life and death—it's much more important than that.

Bill Shankly, UK footballer and manager

Dishonest exam practices can have an effect not only on the culprits but on the institution as a whole, especially if they involve members of a sporting team. In one such case, twelve footballers, along with three athletes and fifteen others were suspended for academic dishonesty at a southern university.

One of the footballers reportedly said that 'cheating is so widespread that you'd have to be a nun not to be involved. Cheating goes on all the time—there's cheating all over the school. Everyone knows it.' He revealed that most of the 77 students in a geography course had looked at notes passed throughout the auditorium during their final exam. In an apparent attempt to justify his actions, he added that 'notes were flying around the room. They were coming from all over. It was scary. We didn't plan to do it; it just happened. There were two people watching about a hundred students. It was too tempting.'

The professor who taught the class, and reported the students after examining their test results, said he believed cheating was widespread on campus. However, the dean of students and the school's interim chancellor disagreed and expressed the view that cheating reports were exaggerated.

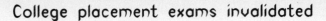

College placement exams invalidated

If a thing's worth doing, it's worth doing badly.

G. K. Chesterton

If there is a suspicion of widespread cheating in an examination, the drastic solution is to cancel all results and have every candidate resit the paper. This unfortunately punishes those who were innocent. Moreover, those responsible for administering the exam may have caused the problem in the first place.

In one incident, college placement examinations taken by seventy-nine students at a high school were invalidated by the Educational Testing Service (ETS) after school officials discovered that seven students had cheated on their exams. The ETS put the blame on the high school officials who failed to properly monitor students taking the tests. In an unpopular measure, all those students seeking credit for college courses in biology, American history and English composition were required to retake the tests during the summer vacation.

Difficulties arose when it was discovered that students at the school were seated too close together and that an inadequate number of supervisors was present in the examination room. ETS guidelines stated that students should have been separated by five feet and that there should have been three invigilators allocated for between 51 and 100 students. In this instance, only one supervisor was present and students were seated next to each other and separated by dividers.

Cheating in mathematics exam uncovered

Stand firm in your refusal to remain conscious during algebra. In real life, I assure you, there is no such thing as algebra.

Fran Lebowitz, Social Studies, *1981*

The principal of a high school in Queens once cancelled the results of a Board of Regents exam in mathematics after determining that at least 20 per cent of the pupils who took the test could have cheated. He revealed that a school custodian found photocopies of the test along with an answer key on the front lawn of the school a few minutes after pupils began taking the exam. During the examination itself, a supervisor discovered a student with a crib sheet of the answers.

During the test, the principal announced over the school's public address system that the photocopies had been found and later detected that 100 of 504 test scores were significantly better than the students' course grades. He said: 'The kids were aware that we knew about the stolen exam and if we did nothing we would have given the wrong message to them.'

This episode followed the state cancellation of the Regents exams in chemistry after the *New York Post* published the answer key to the stolen exam. With evidence of widespread cheating, the state gave individual schools and districts the authority to void the tests, after discovering copies of the exams and answers were being sold. The *Post* claimed that thousands of bootleg copies of answers to various Regents exams were being sold for up to $2000 per copy.

Assignment substitution

Never underestimate a man who overestimates himself.

Franklin D. Roosevelt

Lecturers must be careful when collecting written home-work from students. It is inviting trouble to let students simply place their completed work in an open box that is accessible to anybody. Some students would be tempted to copy the answers from other papers in the box and in some cases even steal the paper copied from altogether so that the marker will be unaware of any cheating.

Something similar occurred at a southern university when an undergraduate strolled into the room where he was supposed to submit a ten-page final paper for his English course. Not only didn't he have an assignment to hand in, but he could not even be bothered copying the work of somebody else—that would have been too time consuming and easy for the examiners to detect. Instead, he simply reached into the pile for another student's paper, erased the name on it, and substituted his own name.

An assistant dean who recalled the incident later said that 'the other student obtained a zero and this student was awarded the good grade'. Fortunately, in this instance the substitution was discovered and the correct grades awarded. The culprit was suspended from school.

It was also reported that about 100 other students were punished for cheating each year, but most cases were never passed on to university officials for disciplinary action. As a result, officials at the institution approved a new honour code; an innovation for a public university with as many as 36 000 students on its campus.

Board member arrested

You'll never find a rich acupuncturist—they only work for pin money.
Anon.

For some students, the only way around a lack of academic ability is either to cheat in some way or to gain assistance from course authorities. In some cases this means bribing either the person who sets the exam paper to reveal the questions beforehand or—perhaps even more astutely—the individual responsible for marking.

An investigation involving large amounts of money was mounted when officials reported that a member of a state acupuncture licensing board was arrested on suspicion of taking payments of close to $1 million from applicants in exchange for answers to test questions. The students involved were applying for certification from the state Acupuncture Examining Committee.

It was alleged that the offender had solicited and received bribes ranging between $10 000 and $20 000 from at least eighty prospective acupuncturists. He was booked on suspicion of bribery and held in prison in place of $5000 bail.

Medical students accused

My doctor is wonderful. Once in 1955 when I couldn't afford an operation, he touched up the X-rays.
Joey Bishop, US comedian

The medical profession came under the microscope when the head of the Association of Medical Colleges was reported as saying that dramatic cases of researchers falsifying data were just a small part of the lapsing integrity of the medical world. He stated:

A sleaze factor has crept into science and medicine. It begins with the premedical environment. Students are 'study machines' who are characterised as hypercompetitive, narrow minded, greedy and dishonest at best, and 'ferocious geeks' at worst.

The head also said that undergraduate cheating and faked letters of recommendation were far too common, and that during a ten-year period the association had investigated 952 cases of suspected dishonesty in applications for medical school.

In one instance, investigators found that students had stolen supplies of paper on which grade transcripts were printed. In another incident, a student actually enrolled at two different medical schools, letting his academically inferior roommate impersonate him at one.

A survey revealed that two-thirds of United States medical schools reported that cheating was a concern and a study at one school showed that between 33 and 48 per cent of students admitted to cheating as undergraduates while 17 per cent admitted to cheating as medical students.

Impersonator racket uncovered

Moral indignation is jealousy with a halo.

H. G. Wells

One of the better-known cheating techniques is to have an impostor sit the examination on your behalf, although it is now becoming a risky business with the introduction of digitised photo identity cards which are extremely difficult to alter. For the impostor it may seem like the chance to make quick money, with the amounts on offer often being dependent on the difficulty of the subject.

However, substitutions occur even at school as highlighted by the case of one high school student who said he took a Scholastic Aptitude Test (SAT) for a student at a different school because he wanted to make 'an easy $300'. Another student claimed to have turned down a $500 offer to take the test for the 'friend of a friend'.

According to students at these schools, impersonators were not uncommon at standardised test centres. One anonymous student was quoted as saying that 'I don't, like, have many morals. I don't like people that much and I don't really mind prostituting myself. It was good money so I did it.'

The going rate for an impersonator was revealed to be between $250 and more than $1000. An enterprising student who started up a SAT tutoring service claimed that three people asked him to take the test for them. One offered him $1500 since he was 'feeling a lot of pressure from his family to get into a good school'. The tutor did not enter into the spirit of things and refused the offers.

The executive director of the SAT program said that if a test looks suspicious then officials go back and compare the signature on the registration form with the signature on the test itself. He added that the Educational Testing Service (ETS) cancels 1000 scores a year out of two million nation-wide for 'security reasons'.

Sex cheats

All teaching in all subjects aims to stimulate interest. It would be odd if this were not true of sex lessons.

Roger Probert, Birmingham headmaster, 1973

School officials reported that a final examination held in a western state university's largest class, a human sexuality course with about 700 students, had its marks cancelled because some students were caught cheating. The university student discipline officer revealed that at least ten students were caught taking into the exam duplicate papers that were marked with the correct answers.

When the scheme was uncovered, the test was stopped and declared void by the teacher who said, 'I guess they don't want to run home and flunk sex'. Some students told school officials that copies of the test had been circulating around campus for about a week before the exam, with one student claiming that copies were being openly sold by somebody operating from a car.

The teacher summed up the situation nicely by commenting that 'many students come to this course thinking they know everything about human sexuality. They find out they don't, so they find an easy way out.'

Exam substitution leads to community service

I don't want a lawyer to tell me what I cannot do. I hire him to tell me how to do what I want to do.

J. Pierpont Morgan

There was a bizarre exam substitution case involving a law school graduate who had failed the state bar exam and then allowed his more academically gifted wife to sit for the test in his place. As a result, he was placed on three years probation and ordered to perform 500 hours of community service.

The Superior Court judge refrained from jailing the student after his attorney successfully argued that the defendant's life was already 'in a shambles' and 'perhaps irreparably damaged' as a result of the case. His by now ex-wife was placed on probation after pleading no contest to two counts of false impersonation, while the conviction was later reduced to a misdemeanour.

The prosecutor reportedly said that the pregnant wife had aroused curiosity at the test site by wearing an identification tag containing a photograph in which she tried to appear masculine. The photo pictured her wearing a button-down shirt with her hair pulled back and eyebrows pencilled.

Although the case was spread over two years, it did not resolve the question as to whether it was the husband or the wife who engineered the scheme. The couple were by then already divorced.

Registration fraud scheme

If you have to tell them who you are, you aren't anybody.
Gregory Peck

It's bad enough that students find the need to cheat in an exam to improve their performance, but some even go one step further and use illegal tactics to enter the course in the first place. In one case, officials at a northern state university revealed that up to 200 students could have been involved in a phoney registration scheme for high-demand courses in the spring semester.

The university vice-president said the fraudulent scheme apparently began when a handful of students obtained registration stamps for courses such as economics, sociology, psychology and pre-business. They used these to illegally authorise hundreds of admissions to classes, on some occasions charging $10 for the service. He added that:

> we've never had an incident of this magnitude in the past. Students have argued to me in meetings that have been held that this has gone on for a long time and why are we reacting so negatively to this

incident. But we are certainly not aware of this sort of widespread problem on campus.

The university detected the phoney registration cards when the communication studies department, which offered several high-demand courses, noticed large numbers of extra students appearing in classes that were already full. It would have been impossible for the students to have been added legally to the class list because clerks close entry to the class once all slots are filled. Some unfortunate students were caught by admitting themselves to classes that had already been cancelled.

OTHER COUNTRIES

Schoolgirls exposed

I used to be Snow White but I drifted.

Mae West (attrib.)

There was an intriguing report in June 1995 from Radio France Internationale regarding the dishonest activities of high school girls in Nigeria. It seemed that examination cheating had become so widespread in secondary schools that strong preventative measures were required to stamp it out.

In an intrepid move, examination supervisors insisted that school girls remove their underwear before entering the exam room, presumably to ensure that no illegal material was smuggled in. It was not revealed who actually checked whether the girls obeyed orders or indeed whether they had found other places to hide their crib sheets. Moreover, in an attempt to maintain equality of the sexes, it would be expected that males should also remove their underpants, although there were no immediate reports on this.

Leaking papers run to milk bars

Too bad that all the people who know how to run the country are busy driving taxi cabs or cutting hair.

George Burns

The activities of students cheating the exam system can have a rebound effect even on politicians who must sometimes shoulder the blame. In June 1992, an Algerian education minister resigned after the government decided to cancel the Baccalaureate science examinations for university entrance after a massive leak of exam questions. This resulted from the claim of some students that advance copies of papers could be picked up at hairdressers and local milk bars.

If it became necessary, the new minister had the power to call on the defence ministry to stop exam cheating in the re-sit of papers by over 160 000 school students. In an attempt to avoid a repetition of the previous disaster, the government promised heavy punishment for anyone involved with the leaking of the new papers.

How to stay inconspicuous

Silence is one of the hardest arguments to refute.
Josh Billings, US humorist

A teacher at a school in Saudi Arabia revealed that students in an English language test used a variety of techniques to improve exam performance. In an amusing incident, a student carefully pre-recorded information on a tape recorder hidden in his pocket and, using a very thin wire, connected it to a miniature earpiece.

This particular method is not all that innovative, but the culprit soon discovered that choosing the right moment to cheat is vital. In his excitement at using the device, he inadvertently disconnected the wire from its socket in the recorder, at which point it played his crib notes at full volume through the normal speakers. The ear-splitting volume immediately attracted the attention of the entire examination hall including the supervisors.

A more creative student who was also well versed in cheating activities revealed that he regularly ate a quantity of onions and garlic for breakfast to keep invigilators away from him during the exam. Apparently this practice had worked quite successfully on a number of occasions.

Protest across the water

He hasn't an enemy in the world—but all his friends hate him.
          Eddie Cantor, The Chase and Sanborn Hour, *NBC Radio, 1933*

Heated accusations were reportedly exchanged across the Jordan River in July 1991 over the disruption of annual school matriculation examinations for Palestinians in the occupied West Bank by 'cheating, acrimony and violence'. The exams, known as the *tawjihi*, are set by the Jordanian Ministry of Education and were ordered to be postponed after reports of widespread copying and intimidation of invigilators by activists.

However, Israel's military authorities insisted that the exams should proceed and it was left to the Jordanian officials to decide which exams should be resat. These included one biology and two English papers.

In one incident, pistols and knives were produced during an English exam and teachers were warned not to intervene while pupils systematically copied answers from each other. In some cases, cars with loudspeakers were used to shout out correct answers in the streets outside school premises.

Do me a favour

She's the original good time that was had by all.
          Bette Davis, of another actress (attrib.)

In an innovative move, the Education Minister of the Ivory Coast decided to launch a campaign to crackdown on 'gymslip Lolitas' who offer sexual favours in return for good marks. He declared that 'it is disturbing and morally indefensible to see educators having "special relations" with their female pupils. They are committing intellectual incest with the result being unwanted pregnancies and dangerous abortions.'

It was reported that many Ivorians knew of teachers or even university professors who slept with their students on the promise of good exam marks. Some girls were described as 'enthusiastic victims, using their charms to avoid study'. The Ivorian society has no precedent for girls taking legal action against teachers on the grounds of sexual harassment.

In addition to coping with sexual problems, one teacher commented that 'at the back of my class the children smoke, play cards and read magazines and the general overseers are unable to control the situation'. Another lamented, 'I have more than 100 pupils in my class. The benches are so close together that to get from one side of the classroom to the other I have to climb over them.'

Indeed, student riots have prompted some African countries to declare entire academic years null and void. The Cameroon teacher's union vice-president revealed that examiners, invigilators and teachers are involved in 'all sorts of bargaining with the pupils'.

The overcrowding and bribery problems are exemplified by Abidjan's university, built thirty years ago for 6000 students but now having to cope with an enrolment of 50 000.

Time rolls on

Television is more interesting than people. If it were not, we should have people standing in the corners of our rooms.

Alan Coren, The Times

It must be admitted that many students are successful in their efforts to cheat the system, and that one of the common methods of catching them is to rely on the honesty of others.

In Saudi Arabia, one conscience-stricken high school student recently decided to turn in his fellow classmates who, he claimed, regularly cheated in their exams.

He revealed that one of their favourite tactics was to remove the mechanisms from their watches and replace them with a roll of paper on which they had written any information which they felt might come in handy. This was sometimes known as 'making a television' since the changed watch face resembled a small screen.

The roll of paper was inserted between two disks that could be wound forward or backwards. This enabled the students to review the information on the roll 'as though watching television'. In most countries it is rare to check watches before an examination, although in light of this confession it might be a good idea.

An alternative use for underwear

Brevity is the soul of lingerie.

Dorothy Parker (attrib.)

When a student is caught red-handed cheating during an exam, there can be a variety of different emotions involved. These could include a quiet resignation or anger on the part of the culprit, or a feeling of triumph or disappointment for the accuser.

In an odd case involving underwear, extreme evasive measures were taken by a twenty-year-old female student who was caught cheating in an examination at a university in Cairo. The unfortunate woman, who was studying in the faculty of Arabic and Islamic studies, was reportedly found with a crib sheet hidden under her bra, although it was not known exactly how the supervisor managed to uncover the evidence.

In a moment of panic the distraught culprit ran to the open window and leapt out. It was plain bad luck that the exam was held on the fifth floor of the building, with the outcome being that she suffered severe injuries. She was immediately rushed to hospital with several broken bones.

Cheating is normal

One of the few lessons I have learned in life is that there is invariably something odd about women who wear ankle socks.

Alan Bennett, The Old Country, *1978*

According to a report in June 1994, a Polish educator said that 'cheating is an industry' in classrooms in Poland. One student vividly described how high school girls wore *sciegawka* (cheat sheets) above their knees under their stockings. To access the sheets, they crossed their legs and inched their skirts up their thighs so they could peek at answers during the exam. Such gestures also provided concentration difficulties for some of the males sitting nearby.

During an oral exam, a university student smuggled in technical information on cards so small that he could cup them in the palm of his hand and refer to them if necessary. Although he was caught and severely reprimanded by one of the examiners for cheating, a second examiner also admonished him for a different reason. His complaint was that the student had the audacity to cheat during his orals, whereas most candidates apparently just cheated on written exams.

The majority of students admitted that cheating was widespread but dismissed it as a 'natural occurrence'. For some it's just 'friends helping friends' or insurance for a passing grade, with one student claiming that they were required to learn excessive amounts of useless, detailed information—a system that 'makes us cheat'. Others expressed the view that some exams were simply too difficult to pass without cheating and that anyone who refused to cheat was considered a 'goody-two-shoes'.

One Polish instructor who finally became fed up with cheating caught a university student red-handed and sent her out of the classroom. Later he confessed, 'I felt really bad. I was wet with sweat and she was crying.' Indeed, he thought the ambiguous policies on cheating should result in some degree of tolerance.

Arrangements cancelled

Everybody who is incapable of learning has taken to teaching—that is really what our enthusiasm for education has come to.
Oscar Wilde, The Decay of Lying, *1889*

In a scandal involving teachers, the Education Minister of Haifa decided to invalidate the matriculation exams in political science, economics and civics undertaken at a certain high school. He did so because of the extraordinary situation whereby, because of a special 'arrangement', pupils were allowed to write notes to teachers asking questions during the test.

While many students elsewhere would find the situation appealing, the government was not amused and also reprimanded the school's principal for instituting the procedure which had definitely not been approved by the ministry. In addition, the school's matriculation exams supervisor was relieved of duties for the rest of the year.

The arrangement came to light when an 'anti-cheating' investigative team from the ministry made an unexpected visit to the school and found the notes. The principal, who still apparently saw nothing wrong with the scheme, said, 'we didn't hide the notes because we didn't think we had any reason'.

Headdress hides radio

Radio has no future.

Lord Kelvin, President of the Royal Society, 1897

Some students seem capable of concealing crib notes on almost any part of the body, but a novel approach surfaced in Jordan when an Arab schoolboy used his headdress to advantage. His attire became the receptacle for concealing a matchbox-sized radio communication device that he used to make contact with a friend outside. It was reported that the boy aroused suspicion during the secondary school exams at Zarqa, near Amman, when he asked to go to the toilet several times saying he felt sick. A subsequent search by a suspicious supervisor revealed the tiny two-way radio tucked in his headdress.

Enquiries uncovered a plot whereby the villain had been using the transmitter to get advice on how to answer exam questions from a friend in a car parked outside the examination centre. However, it was quickly pointed out that the boy was not a Jordanian national but came from 'a neighbouring Arab country'.

Loudhailers used to broadcast exam answers

Are you going to come quietly or do I have to use ear-plugs?

Spike Milligan, The Goon Show, *BBC Radio*

Learning from past experience, brave, forward-planning police formed temporary anti-cheating squads in parts of Egypt in June 1987 as high school students prepared for year-end exams. Their action resulted from reports of teachers being beaten up, examination papers stolen and outside loudhailers broadcasting answers to students taking exams.

These activities were all part of a cheating scandal that was exposed when an examination committee charged that parents in the town of Al-Husseniya banded together to give their intermediate school children, aged twelve to fifteen, the answers to their exams. In one case a man broke into a school room while students were sitting an exam and ran out. Within minutes, answers to the questions were being broadcast into the room from loudspeakers outside. A few minutes later thugs broke into the school and distributed model answers to the students.

In another incident, it was only after authorities threatened to carry out a body search that about 500 out of 2000 students at Zigzag University in Upper Egypt owned up to having crib sheets. Severe pressure is placed on the students since a university degree is the minimum requirement for a white-collar job and their future depends on their aggregate marks. Hence both students and parents are greatly tempted to cheat in order to gain as high a mark as possible.

In an understandable move, teachers admitted they had turned a blind eye to mass cheating for fear of being beaten up. One tutor said, 'We teachers say our prayers every morning before going to examinations because we don't know whether we will return home safely or be carried on stretchers to hospital.'

More good books from Allen & Unwin
on the following pages . . .

GET GREAT MARKS FOR YOUR ESSAYS
John Germov

NOT SURE HOW TO BEGIN WRITING UNIVERSITY ESSAYS?
FOUR ESSAYS TO WRITE AND ONLY FOUR WEEKS TO GO
BEFORE THE DEADLINE? THEN THIS IS THE BOOK FOR YOU.

Find out the rules of the essay writing game, how to
muckrake for information, write drafts, handle references
and do analysis. Discover where you win and lose marks.
Learn how to take the right short cuts and make the most
of your time.

Get Great Marks for Your Essays tells you all you need to
know to write essays in the Humanities and Social Sciences.

*'This guide to essay writing is great. I had a lot of
trouble passing my essays. After reading this book I
found I wasn't alone. This book has helped me to
understand how to improve my writing . . . It's easy to
read and pretty cool too!'*

— *Student comment*

John Germov is a lecturer in Sociology at the University
of Newcastle and has taught study skills to first year
students for many years.

ISBN 1 86448 158 7

HI FI DAYS
Craig Mathieson

MOVE OVER MIDNIGHT OIL, JIMMY BARNES AND INXS.
NEW KIDS ON THE BLOCK—SILVERCHAIR, YOU AM I AND
SPIDERBAIT—ARE JUST THREE OF THE YOUNG BANDS
MAKING IT BIG IN AUSTRALIA AND OVERSEAS.

silverchair's impact both here and in the United States has
been phenomenal and *Juice* editor, Craig Mathieson, is one
of the few members of the press to extensively interview
the elusive group. The result is a unique in depth look at
this record-breaking young Newcastle band, which places
them within the context of the explosion of talent on the
Australian music scene. In this funky fanzine-style book,
Craig Mathieson goes on the road with these three key
bands and interviews their members.

Craig Mathieson was born in 1971 and he has been
writing professionally about rock and roll since the age of
eighteen. In that time he has nearly completed a Bachelor
of Arts in Journalism while contributing to daily papers and
rock magazines both here and overseas. At the age of 23
he became the editor of *Juice* magazine, one of Australia's
leading pop culture magazines. *Hi Fi Days* is his first book.

Illustrations

ISBN 1 86448 232 X

POSTCARDS FROM THE NET
Jon Casimir

WANT TO FIND THE SPOT—NOT THE G ONE, **THE** ONE?
OR FIND MR PUDDY'S HOMESITE? OR THE HOME OF THE
UNDEAD? OR WOULD YOU RATHER SEARCH OUT PORN
(BE WARNED—GOING TO THE NEWSAGENT'S WILL BE
MUCH QUICKER). MORE TO THE POINT, WOULD YOU LIKE
TO BE TOLD NOT JUST HOW TO USE THE NET BUT WHY
YOU SHOULD AND WHERE YOU CAN GO?

In this zappy, up-to-the minute guide, intrepid Net traveller
Jon Casimir reports back from the sites he finds and
explores the issues—some serious, some not—raised by the
explosion in Net culture.

Postcards from the Net is not nerdy or bogged down in
Net lingo, and you won't have to be eighteen or under to
read it. It is written from an Australian perspective for an
Australian audience—rather than assuming we are all,
already, part of one big global family. An ambient mix of
the discursive and resourseful, this book is the perfect
guide for those who have just begun to think about taking
the trip into cyberspace, as well as an invaluable resource
tool and inspiration for those already out there 'surfing'.

John Casimir writes on popular culture and technology
for the *Sydney Morning Herald*. He has been published in
most major Australian newspapers and magazines and is a
regular Mr Rent-an-Opinion on ABC Radio.

Illustrations

ISBN 1 86448 233 8

DIY FEMINISM
Edited by Kathy Bail

FEMINISM IS NOT A DIRTY WORD FOR TWENTYSOMETHING WOMEN; IT OFFERS AN OUTLOOK THAT IS PART OF AN OVERALL DO-IT-YOURSELF STRATEGY.

Recently characterised in the media by an older generation of feminists as an often puritanical, narrow-minded generation, this collection shows that young women are in fact streetsmart, engaged and in-yer-face. Here a diverse group of riot grrrls, lipstick lesbians, femocrats, musicians, writers, artists and comedians interpret feminism broadly and confidently, with direct reference to their own experiences. Taking feminist social and political outlooks in their stride, these nineties survival strategies use everything from a wicked sense of humour to a detailed knowledge of the legal system.

Contributors include: Lisbeth Gorr, Rosie Cross, Natasha Stott Despoja, Rebecca Cox, VNS Matrix, Fotini Epanomitis, Ashley Hay, Cathy Wilcox and Kaz Cooke.

Kathy Bail is a Sydney-based journalist and has worked as deputy editor of *Cinema Papers* and as a senior writer at *The Independent*. She is now the editor of *Rolling Stone* magazine.

Illustrations

ISBN 1 86448 231 1

RETURNING TO LEARNING

STUDYING AS AN ADULT: TIPS, TRAPS AND TRIUMPHS
Caroline Brem

SO, YOU'RE GETTING BACK INTO STUDY FOR THE FIRST
TIME IN A WHILE? MAYBE A TAFE OR COMMUNITY CENTRE
COURSE, A DEGREE, OR AN OPEN LEARNING OR EXTERNAL
COURSE FROM A UNIVERSITY? IT'S A CHALLENGE! BUT ONE
THAT YOU'RE UP TO, WITH THE RIGHT APPROACH.

The experience will be very different from your years at
school. Life is no longer so simple. You'll have to juggle
your time and commitments, keep up relationships with
family and friends, create space and energy for learning,
and cope with new approaches to teaching. There's a lot
going on, but with planning and commitment, and a little
help from this book, you'll get the most out of your study.

In this inspirational guide, Caroline Brem addresses the
needs and concerns of all those who are returning to
learning. She gives entertaining and, above all, useful
advice on:
- your attitude to learning
- setting up the environment for study and learning
- tips on your time, space, health and relationships
- overcoming blocks to learning and finding that mental
  energy
- the resources, skills and study techniques you need, and
- all the fiddly bits of essays, reports and exams.

Caroline Brem teaches philosophy of education,
communication skills, English as a second language and
adult learning theory at university and TAFE level. Her
previous book, *Are We On The Same Team Here?*, has been
admired throughout the Asia Pacific region for its
sympathetic approach to team activity at work and in the
community.

ISBN 1 86448 071 8